Incorporating the Familiar
An Investigation into Legal Sensibilities in Nunavik

Focusing on the delivery of justice in Inuit communities in northern Quebec, *Incorporating the Familiar* investigates the complexities and contradictions of accommodation between Aboriginal and non-Aboriginal legal systems. Conflict between the two legal orders, Susan Drummond argues, is really about incommensurability between underlying cultural codes. She uses legal pluralism as a springboard to reflect on wider questions of intercultural history, concepts of identity and belonging, and problems of communication across cultures and between men and women.

Drummond examines philosophic, ethnographic, and legal dilemmas produced by the interaction between legal cultures, setting up a dialogue between narrative and theory by interspersing accounts of her field experiences in Inuit communities with analytical chapters. In the first section she addresses problems of delivery of justice in Nunavik and explores the cultural determinacy of understanding. In the second section she focuses on the problem of family violence and the complexities to which it gives rise in rendering justice in the north of Québec. In the third section she provides an ethnographic account of Nunavik's first sentencing circle, underlining her contention that juridical rules emerge from the habits and way of life of a society.

Exploring the quandaries of intercultural communication and contemplating how diverse legal sensibilities might be mutually recognized, *Incorporating the Familiar* evokes the possibilities and limits of intercultural accommodation.

SUSAN DRUMMOND is a doctoral candidate in the Faculty of Law, McGill University.

Incorporating the Familiar

An Investigation into Legal Sensibilities in Nunavik

SUSAN G. DRUMMOND

McGill-Queen's University Press

Montreal & Kingston · London · Buffalo

Legal deposit fourth quarter 1997
Bibliothèque nationale du Québec

Printed in Canada on acid-free paper

This book has been published with the help of a grant from
the Humanities and Social Sciences Federation of Canada,
using funds provided by the Social Sciences and Humanities
Research Council of Canada.

McGill-Queen's University Press acknowledges the support
received for its publishing program from the Canada
Council's Block Grants program.

Canadian Cataloguing in Publication Data

Drummond, Susan G. (Susan Gay), 1959–
  Incorporating the familiar : an investigation into legal
  sensibilities in Nunavik
  Includes bibliographical references.
  ISBN 0-7735-1671-9
  1. Inuit – Legal status, laws, etc. – Quebec (Province) –
  Nunavik. 2. Justice, Administration of – Quebec (Province) –
  Nunavik. 3. Ethological jurisprudence. 4. Culture conflict –
  Quebec (Province) – Nunavik. I. Title.
  KEQ1060.D78 1997   306.2´5´0899712071411   C97-900716-X

Typeset in Minion 10.5/13
by Caractéra inc., Quebec City

For Jean-Marc and Noah,
compagnons de route

Contents

Acknowledgments

I am grateful to Jeremy Webber for his diligent supervision of my legal and intellectual career, for his generous support of this project, and for his human decency.

Thanks to Louisa Whiteley and Eva Lepage for their interpretations of Nunavik, and to Stan Kudek for his perspicuous introduction to the field of inquiry.

Thanks to Jeremy Webber, Peter Leonard, James Tully, Roderick Macdonald Natalie Oman, Dale Turner, Cressida Hayes, Elizabeth Urtnowski, Kristen Norget, Blaine Baker, and Keith Drummond for reading and commenting upon earlier drafts of the manuscript. The scrupulous commentary of the anonymous readers for the press and the sensitive copyediting of Maureen Garvie are also appreciated.

Thanks to my parents, for the obvious and the obscure.

Funding for the research for this book was provided by the Fonds pour la Formation de Chercheurs et l'Aide à la Recherche, Association of Canadian Universities for Northern Studies, Max Bell Fellowship, McGill University's School of Social Work, McGill University's Faculty of Law, McGill's Northern Training Fellowship, John Peacock Memorial Fellowship, Social Sciences and Humanities Research Council of Canada, McGill Centre for Teaching and Research on Women, and Japanese/ Menonnite Foundation of Canada.

Circuit Court/
Circus Court

Tigujaumaju: Inuktitut word for
1) being taken away by an uncontrollable force;
used for 2) when someone goes to prison.
(Definition provided by Louisa Whiteley,
Inuk co-researcher; June 1992)

In the summer of 1992, I flew to Kuujjuaq for four months to begin fieldwork for a joint degree in law and social work. After working in Kuujjuaq's battered women's shelter for a fews weeks, I arranged with the director of social services to begin qualitative research on family violence in the community. He hired Louisa Whiteley, an Inuk who was then twenty-one years old, to work with me.

Louisa and I began by calling into being a community group to sponsor our research. This group was composed of approximately twenty residents of Kuujjuaq who had professional or personal experience with family violence. For this group we produced a report, *Family Violence in Kuujjuaq: Talking to Each Other*, based on local interviews. Several people shared private tales of violence. Two of these stories appear later in this book.

As part of our investigation, we attended the June session of the circuit court, which forms the basis of the following account. The cases here recounted took place over two court sessions in the week of 15 June 1992. I have rearranged the cases so that they read as having taken place at the same sitting. There were a small number of other cases on the docket that evening. Apart from these liberties, the material is as faithful to the actual events as my fieldnotes permit. I have taken the liberty of changing the names of those who came before the court.

The circuit court is also known as the itinerant court. The Inuit have been known to call the court the "flying circus" or "circus court." This characterization is not appreciated by those who work with court. In a memo submitted to the minister of Justice in 1986, the court noted that "the expression 'flying circus' greatly affects the different people involved with the court. The comparison with public entertainers is no longer found amusing by anyone and those most involved do not have the intention of seeing it perpetuated" (author's translation).[1]

The format of the narrative invites the reader to engage in an interpretive process similar to the one in which the ethnographer is involved. The material calls for recurrent repositioning as the reader goes about understanding what is presented, adjusting an emerging set of questions throughout the course of the reading in light of counter-factual material from other points in time, space, and perspective until uncertainty diminishes and one gets a feel for how to go on.

Read the main text all the way through at once and then return to the subtext, or read it concurrently with the subtexts trailing in all directions. To choose the first option is to irretrievably forgo the immediate sense of dissonance of the second approach. Yet to read the texts concurrently precludes the state of innocence suggested by reading the main text straight through. The reader might also approach the material from another direction altogether. There is a choice to be made, and not one absolutely right way to go on from here … and yet some readings will be off course.

What follows is the direction my experiences suggested to me.

THE ITINERANT COURT

KUUJJUAQ, NUNAVIK
THURSDAY, 18 JUNE 1992

It is still cold in Kuujjuaq. I am still wearing my winter coat, mitts, and boots. The snow that is left on the edge of the gravel road is dirty brown, mixed with blowing sand. On Sunday evening, two days after the court has returned south, the last snow of the season will begin to fall. I have been in Kuujjuaq for one and a half months now.

Kuujjuaq in northern Québec on the Ungava coast is the largest Inuit settlement north of the 55th parallel and is Nunavik's administrative centre. At the time of the June circuit, roughly 1,400 people lived in Kuujjuaq. Approximately 1,100 were Inuit. The majority of the non-Inuit were Québécois. Inuit from smaller communities consider Kuujjuaq large, chaotic, and metropolitan.

The circuit court flies from Val d'Or to Nunavik approximately every five weeks. It sits on the Ungava coast for a five-day week. There are eight communities scattered along the roughly 900 miles that make up the Ungava coastline. The court sat in Kuujjuaq for three days. Because of the brevity of the court's stay, hearings are held all day and into the night. It is daylight as I walk to the courtroom at seven in the evening.

The lawyers, social-service workers and probation officer complain of the harried court schedule. When I interviewed a legal-aid lawyer the previous week, he invited me out for a beer at the hotel bar when the court finished up. (This was precluded by the court's overloaded schedule.)

He said that on the final night of their stay, the court officials go to the bar to unwind. He would show me how crazy the bar gets. He has had Inuit women come up to him in the bar and make frank proposals. ("Hey white man. Want to go fuck?")

The summer I was in Kuujjuaq, the hotel bar was the only place where alcohol could be legally purchased. There was also a healthy bootleg market. The bar was often talked of in sensational whispers among the non-Inuit as a spectacle of Inuit debauchery. It, and its ambience, were occasionally alluded to as justification for non-Inuit administrators in the North. The bar, and alcohol generally, were often cited as explanatory factors in interviews I had done in the community on family violence.

This afternoon's hearing was a lengthy youth protection case from which I (and the general public) was excluded. I have been informed by the probation officer that if I return in the evening I should be able to get an idea of what happens in adult court.

At the door of the building there are two Inuit men in their early twenties, smoking. I assume they are waiting for the court to begin as it is unusual to see people waiting outside this building on regular days.

Louisa told me that as the court personnel are only in the North for brief periods of time and only deal with those Inuit who are in conflict with the law, they have a skewed perception of the Inuit.

The probation officer elected to initiate me into an insider's view on the North. I had interviewed him the previous week. He had told me, in conspiratorial tones, that I would get a good idea of what happens in the North from attending court that week as a couple of interesting assault cases were on the docket.

A former RCMP officer, he has worked and lived in Kuujjuaq for two years. His mandate covers probation orders for the whole of the Ungava coast. At the time of the interview he was the sole probation officer for the region.

He claimed to have a special relationship with the Inuit and attributed this to the facts that he is English and that he hunts with them.

During our interview, he was emphatic that Pauktuutit (the Inuit Women's Association of Canada) advocated that to assist in the Inuit quest for sovereignty, Inuit women should have as many children as possible and should stop having abortions. He could not find the document that supported this thesis when I asked him how he had come to this understanding.

He recounted his shock that nobody in the community did anything after a child drowned. The mayor had not gone on the radio and denounced the mother for leaving the child unattended. He had told me this story to underline fundamental and incomprehensible differences between Inuit and non-Inuit. Louisa was astonished when I relayed to her his interpretation of the drowning: Why would anyone seek to enhance the mother's grief?

On one of the court days, while we waited for the courtroom to open, the probation officer informed me that the session was being held up because the social service workers (90 per cent Inuit) never

The courtroom is housed in a one-storey administrative building. It sits opposite the one-storey police building, which is new and clean. The courtroom building used to be the old hospital before the new one was built in 1981; the old hospital was divided up between a number of services. The courtroom and its cluster of offices now occupy the basement.

Inside on the stairs going down to the courtroom, three Inuit people sit, waiting. I recognize one of the women from the women's shelter. In her mid-forties, she is not a battered woman but has been housed at the shelter with her four children for the last five months, waiting for a house to become available. We say hello to each other. She speaks broken English, Inuktitut being her mother tongue.

The court does not start at 7 P.M., as scheduled. I am not told when the session will begin, so I wait, sometimes sitting alone, sometimes standing in the hallway, talking to different people.

In a space next to and under the stairs are three orange plastic chairs and an ashtray containing cellophane wrappers, an empty cigarette box. A handful of Inuit people wait in this area, sometimes sitting on the chairs, sometimes getting up and leaning against the wall, sometimes going outside to smoke.

Facing this area is an office with a large opening covered with a metal grid. It looks like the reception window of a hospital. The probation officer and provincial police (Sureté du Québec: SQ) officers enter and exit this room, chatting with a woman who appears to have some role in the court. I assume she arranges the docket. I also assume she flies with the court as she does not look familiar to me.

finish their paperwork on time. He informed me that he had the best paperwork in the North and that he had been commended on it by his supervisor. He also told me that, with respect to his recommendations about clients, the judge "treated him like a god."

The Kuujjuaq courthouse is the only permanent one in Nunavik. In other Inuit communities, the court is set up in local community buildings such as the school or community hall. One of the legal aid lawyers informed me that the Inuit public do not attend the court hearings in Kuujjuaq where there is an official forum. In his experience, in communities that hold court in the local school, larger numbers of people attend the trials of local Inuit.

In the hallway leading to the courtroom there are a number of small rooms. On the immediate left is the legal-aid office, bare except for a table and chair. The defence lawyers congregate here as they wait for court to start. At one point, one of the legal-aid lawyers who has been with the court for fifteen years comes out into the hall to talk with me about my work.

As the number of non-Inuit in Kuujjuaq is small enough that their faces become quickly familiar, Qallunaat outsiders and newcomers stand out.

I have heard the Inuit word for non-Inuit people, "Qallunaat," interpreted in various ways. Pauktuutit's document *The Inuit Way: A Guide to Inuit Culture* (1990) defined the word as meaning "'people who pamper their eyebrows' and can imply a people who pamper or fuss with nature, or are of a materialistic nature; greedy." I asked Inuit people in Kuujjuaq what the word meant to them and was told that it was simply a conjunction of two words: eyebrow and stomach, and was intended to connote people who had bushy eyebrows and round stomachs.

The singular of Qallunaat is Qallunak just as the singular of Inuit is Inuk: Qallunaat people, a Qallunak person.

I interviewed one of the legal-aid lawyers in the lawyers' office the previous week. He had just flown up from the South. I was surprised to see him in advance of the court. I was familiar with the criticism that the judge, Crown prosecutor, and defence lawyer often arrive in remote Aboriginal communities on the same plane, contributing, as the Law Reform Commission pointed out, "to the belief that all of those officials are on the same side and have already decided the outcome of upcoming cases, and that the criminal court process is designed solely for the convenience of judges and lawyers" (*Aboriginal Peoples and Criminal Justice: Equality, Respect and the Search for Justice*, Law Reform Commission of Canada [Ottawa, 1991], 56). I marvelled that Québec was responding so efficiently, already taking steps to improve the reputation of justice.

In fact, the legal-aid lawyer had arrived a week early to meet with his clients; he had then flown back to Val d'Or, the administrative centre of the northern justice system, and returned, with the Crown prosecutor and judge, on the court plane the following week.

Next to the legal-aid office is the court-worker office. The court-worker is a thin Inuk woman in her forties. The Inuk translator sits in this room chatting informally with her.

Next to the court-worker office is another room, similar to the legal-aid office, empty but for a wood desk, chairs, and filing cabinet. This room has been turned into a makeshift coffee room with a small coffee machine and an open package of styrofoam cups on top of the filing cabinet. The Qallunaat professionals lounge between this room, the metal grid room, and the lawyers' room, talking, laughing, getting their files in order.

The next room is the Crown prosecuter's office. His door is closed. Occasionally he will call someone into his office. A Qallunak woman in an ornate Inuit parka spends thirty minutes with him. When he has finished interviewing witnesses he opens his door, and the Qallunaat professionals extend their perambulations, moving in and out of his office, talking with him. It is not clear whether the conversations are formal or informal.

The court typically engages a translator for the week that it is in Nunavik. The translators are well-paid workers from the community. They are hired on contract for the most part.

One of the prosecutors told me that this particular translator was excellent. This was the first time that he has been satisfied with a translator. Most of them did not convey the full content of what was said to them; or they did not translate directly, instead prefacing their translation with "He is asking you" or "She says that." This prosecutor has asked for a mistrial or an adjournment on several occasions as he doubted that the accused understood what was being said to him or her.

The probation officer told me that he had been unable to get an Inuk probation officer or translator to work with him, as local candidates feel uncomfortably familiar with the accused and convicted.

I interviewed the Crown prosecutor earlier in the week without Louisa present. He was a tall man, impeccably and expensively attired.

He thought that Inuit generations over eighteen years old were already lost. There was nothing that could be done for them – the only

Across the hall from the Crown prosecutor's room is the judge's chambers. This room has two doors, one entering into the hallway, the other directly into the courtroom. The hallway door is closed. I do not see the judge during the period of the wait.

Along the wall leading to the courtroom is a stand of pamphlets on various subjects pertaining to the legal system. I am the only person who idly flips through them. Skimming them like cereal boxes, I glance at the uniformed Inuit police officer. Staring silently ahead, he stands apart from the Inuit waiting for the court to open. He does not interact with the Qallunaat justice personnel either.

solution was to educate young Inuit. He quoted a Cree woman's appraisal that Indians were not ready for self-government because they were so messed up. He agreed that Natives were not equipped to be self-governing, using this woman's confidence for support: the Indians themselves were in agreement.

When I interviewed him later with Louisa present, he did not make reference to the older generations of Inuit nor to Native self-government. He started to ask Louisa to admit that alcohol was the biggest problem in the North: the Inuit have a hard time expressing their emotions; all of their emotions erupt when they are drunk.

He ended our interview by saying that the Inuit are a very spiritual people. He has great respect for their spirituality. He perceives the Inuit as having an immense inner landscape by which he is captivated.

I found out in a later interview with the prosecutor that the Qallunak woman I saw entering his office was involved with an Inuk man who had assaulted her. She was testifying against him. She was terrified.

In an urban setting, I would be unlikely to run into the Qallunak woman I saw entering his office after gaining such a glimpse into her private life. In Kuujjuaq, self-conscious of my insight, I would pass this woman as she haunted the gravel roads, a child in the hood of her parka.

At the time of the court hearing, there were two Native police officers in Kuujjuaq. There had been a third until he, Simiunie C., was charged with sexual assault. His case is discussed in the text.

The Inuit police officers come from Kuujjuaq and know everyone personally in the community; in particular, they know the accused.

I nod at him as I squat for a moment against the wall. He approaches to introduce himself. He has heard that I am doing research on family violence and wants one of the information packages that I handed out to the other Native police officers. I apologize for the oversight and ask if I can interview him later. He agrees.

Louisa, my fellow researcher, arrives shortly after I do. She shakes hands with the Inuit people on the stairs and at the bottom of the stairs. She knows almost all of them. People ask after her boyfriend. He has driven Louisa to the courthouse on his fourwheeler and then driven off.

I ask Louisa if her boyfriend will be at the court hearing. She says he does not feel right attending. He feels it is an invasion of the privacy of

In one family violence case, an Inuk officer had had to arrest his own father for wife assault. The victim was his mother.

In an interview, one of the Inuit officers told me that he did not think that it would be a good idea for the judge to be an Inuk from the North. Due to the size of the communities the judge would frequently have to run into the people he or she had sentenced. Kuujjuaq has only one bank and three stores.

A source of great discomfort for this officer was that he felt socially isolated in the community. He could not be too friendly with the people with whom he had grown up as he might later have to charge one of them.

Louisa Whiteley is fluently trilingual in English, French, and Inuktitut. It is an anomaly for her generation of Kuujjuaq Inuit to speak French. A unilingual French civil servant, remarking on Louisa's exceptional mastery of this language, told me with some resentment that the Inuit of Kuujjuaq make no attempt to speak French.

At the time of our research, Louisa attended CEGEP in Montreal to study social sciences. This was the third year that she had left Kuujjuaq for the winter months in order to study in the South. At the time, she wanted to be a dental hygienist. Many people, including myself, had been trying to convince her to go to university and get a professional degree. She concluded at the end of our research project that she did not want to study social work because she did not want to know as much about people's private lives as she had come to know over the summer – especially when she has to continue living next to them in the community.

the accused. She remarks a number of times that she has a right to attend the court session, that people in Kuujjuaq do not know that they have a right to attend the court sessions. I do not invoke the language of right to justify my presence here.

Louisa and I join the court translator who is now sitting on the stairs, waiting. They know each other from the community. The translator asks if Louisa has heard that the high school was broken into and vandalized the night before. Louisa voices consternation. Does the translator know who did it? People have a good idea, but there is no proof. Rumour has it that it was teenagers. The translator has heard that the vandals only broke in to steal typewriter corrector fluid to sniff. There have been a number of break-ins along the coast, she informs us, where the culprits have scavenged for solvents and left valuables untouched.

After forty minutes of waiting the court is ready to start, and the probation officer tells me that we can go in if we want. The courtroom door has a small window. It opens on a room with cold white walls absorbing the green hum of fluorescent lights. The floors are grey linoleum. The room's four small windows are high, affording a sight of sky between slats of government-issue venetian blinds. The only adornment, a Québec *fleur-de-lis,* hangs limp in the corner.

As we enter the room I realize that I have seen it before: watching Inuit Broadcasting one night at the women's shelter, I had sat through an Inuktitut program on the court. From what I could understand of

Louisa describes herself as a feminist.

Louisa's boyfriend is a pilot with Air Inuit and has been selected by a Native role model program as the Inuit representative on a national poster campaign. The poster hangs in most administrative buildings in Kuujjuaq. Before coming here, I saw the poster hanging in Native organizations in Montréal.

The Inuit realized in the late 1970s that television imported from the South was overwhelming their sense of themselves. The Inuit Broadcasting Corporation (IBC) was established to represent Inuit life and culture back to the Inuit. During the summer of 1992, the IBC showed about four hours of Inuit and Indian programming every night. Much of the material came from the Northwest Territories. Some of it was local. A great deal of the programming was in Inuktitut. The pace often the show, the documentary was created to familiarize the population with the court. It had shown the court-worker office, the judge, the court in session.

The front centre of the room is occupied by a stark installation of desks arranged in a square. At the head of this square, separated by a few feet, is a raised platform. Three wooden panels enclose a desk and a high-backed grey swivel chair. This will be the judge's chair. To one side, lower down, is a small table with a microphone. This is where the translator will sit. Along the facing wall are two rows of plastic chairs for the audience.

In the square, below the judge, the court clerk will face the audience. The defence and prosecution will face each other. The witness or the accused will stand on the same spot, facing the judge and clerk. When the accused is not facing the judge, he or she will sit in a swivel chair at the defence lawyer's side in a triangle with the judge and witness.

Louisa and I sit in the row of chairs against the wall. Other Inuit people, no more than ten, enter and sit in these chairs.

The legal-aid lawyers enter and sit on the left, flopping their files down on the arborite desks, chatting casually. They all wear suits. The Crown prosecutor enters with his files. He is dressed in an expensive-looking double-breasted suit. I am struck by how odd suits look in this northern context where people wear practical, warm clothing. Apart from these legal personnel, I never see people dressed up in Kuujjuaq.

After we have been sitting in the courtroom for five minutes, a woman in a black jacket and black running shoes enters briskly. She is the court clerk. "All rise," she says, as the judge enters with his files and sits at the raised desk. Once he has seated himself, the court clerk tells us we may be seated.

The judge is also wearing a suit. He strikes me as young for a judge. I remember his face from the Inuit Broadcasting program.

had an amateur feel to it. It was not unusual to see an hour of apparently unedited footage of Inuit ice-fishing or to see a shaky whale hunt in the Northwest Territories and the subsequent feast.

After finishing his pleadings for the week, one of the legal-aid lawyers sat in the audience in jeans and a denim jacket. I asked him why he didn't dress in this manner for court. He claimed that the Bar Associa-

The first case is called. As it starts, I am surprised to hear that the court proceeds in English, even though the lawyers and judge are francophone. As they continue in English, I occasionally find myself concentrating to follow what is said.

The first case, a sexual assault case against Simiunie C., was tried three days earlier with a finding of guilt. The present hearing is for sentencing.

After stating this, the judge tells the accused to stand at the desk and face him. An Inuk with dark skin, the accused is a short, stocky man with cropped black hair that stands neatly off his head. He is wearing a

tion has dress codes and that male lawyers have to wear a suit and tie.

The court clerk was never identified by title in the proceedings. She was, nonetheless, recognizable to me.

One of the translators told me that she had recently suggested to the court that they introduce themselves to everyone. She had been translating for the court with no understanding of the various players – who were the lawyers and what were their assigned tasks, who was judge and what was he or she supposed to do, who was the clerk and what was her or his role. Her suggestion came after a court official solicited her input on what the court should be doing differently.

The chief of police told me in an earlier interview that the judge in this court session has been on the circuit for two years.

I had asked the chief of police about sentencing practices in Nunavik as I had heard that Pauktuutit was launching a court challenge alleging that judges in the Northwest Territories tend to give lenient sentences to offenders found guilty of sexually assaulting Inuit women. This judge, I was told, gives harsh sentences for assault cases. He confided to the police chief that he was becoming cynical, seeing the same offenders come before him over and over again. He worried that his cynicism was affecting his sentencing.

The doctors I had interviewed in the community were under the impression that Inuit women were just beginning, over the last year, to press charges against their abusive partners. They speculated that this judge's reputation for sending violent men to jail for extended periods prompted Inuit women to feel they could get some protection from going to court.

pale blue windbreaker, sweat pants, and hightop running shoes. In taking the stand, he moves quickly, his shoulders bent forward, his back to us. His head is bowed. The judge asks him if he needs a translator. He declines.

The judge asks the legal-aid lawyer to make submissions about sentencing. The lawyer notes that the case is going to appeal and that it will take two years before the case arrives in appeal court. If the man is sentenced for two years and then wins the appeal, he asks, what would happen with the time the accused spent in jail? He notes that the accused has no history of violence. He asks that the judge suspend sentence.

The mother tongue of the Ungava Inuit is, for the most part, Inuktitut. Where it is not Inuktitut, it is, for the most part, English.

I know the accused in the sexual assault. He was one of the Native police officers. Louisa and I had included him on the invitation list for our first community meeting on family violence. When I was delivering the invitations, the shelter coordinator informed me that Simiunie C. had just been charged with sexual assault.

Although we had already printed and sealed the invitations, Louisa insisted that we re-do them all and take his name off the invitation list; otherwise it would injure the credibility of our research. It would make us appear out of touch, as everyone knew he was charged.

When we were preparing the invitations for the second community meeting a month after the court session, the secretary of Social Services, who was typing out the envelopes, informed us that we had forgotten Simiunie C.'s name. We told her that his name had been taken off the list because he had been sentenced to two years of jail for sexual assault.

She informed us that Simiunie was appealing the decision and was back in the community until the appeal hearing. She then told us that he was being hired as a social service worker the next week. Taken aback by our surprise, she offered that she had heard that the victim had made the story up.

When Louisa and I confronted the directors of Social Services and Youth Protection about the hiring of a man who had just been convicted of sexual assault, we were told that the case was on appeal; therefore there was no certainty that he had done the crime. As well, he was the best qualified candidate for the job.

The judge remarks curtly that it is his job to sentence, regardless of whether there is an appeal. Does the legal-aid lawyer have a case indicating that this is not so? The lawyer replies that he does not have one with him. The judge tells him he will give him a recess to find such a case, adding dryly that he doubts he will find one.

The lawyer stands, thanks the judge, and bows. He indicates to Simiunie C. that he should follow him out of the courtroom. On his way out of the room Simiunie looks furtively at Louisa.

The court clerk calls the next case. The accused is not in the room so the clerk calls the name into a microphone. Several moments later the accused enters from the hallway. An old man of more than eighty years, he walks into the room on crutches with an old Inuk woman at his side. He has short white hair and a swatch of black hair at the top of his head. He is wearing billy boots, black wool pants, and a plaid shirt under a down jacket. His lawyer beckons him to sit in the swivel chair. The old Inuk woman sits in the audience, leaning forward on the edge of her chair. The judge asks the accused if he wants a translator. The old man waits while the question is translated. He says something in Inuktitut which is translated back into English. Yes, he wants translation.

Two men in the audience, sitting next to each other, start whispering. When they entered the courtroom with Louisa and me, they walked up to each other with broad smiles and shook each other's hands before sitting down together. The judge stops the proceedings abruptly and tells the men to stop talking. The men look up, startled. I too am startled by the harsh tone of the judge's voice which is louder than what has preceded and sounds cross. One of the men is smiling. The judge asks the smiling man what he is laughing at. The man replies that he was smiling at something someone said. The judge says that there is to be no talking and no laughing in his court. Is that understood? The man stops smiling. Yes, it is understood.

The judge turns back to the old Inuk man and quickly reads out in English a string of offences which include assault. The judge waits while this is translated into Inuktitut and then asks the man whether he is pleading guilty or not guilty. The translator translates this. The old man recounts something in Inuktitut to the translator, who looks confused by the response. She hesitates, then says, "He says something about how his children were not listening to him." The legal-aid lawyer rolls his eyes.

The judge says, "Ask him whether he is pleading guilty or not guilty."

This is translated and the man responds again in Inuktitut, this time at length. The translator says something to him again in Inuktitut. He responds. She again hesitates, looks frustrated, and says in English that the man is saying that he hit his children because they were not listening to him. The judge frowns. He looks at the legal-aid lawyer and asks, with irritation, "Does your client understand what he is being charged with or not?"

The lawyer, standing up, says, "Yes, your honour, my client understands what he is being charged with. I have spent the last half hour discussing this with him. He is apparently uncooperative. He has agreed to plead guilty to the charges. He assured me he understood what he was charged with. Now he is coming up with this."

The judge asks if there had been a translator present. The lawyer begins to raise his voice, saying. "Yes, your honour. There was a translator. The man has had all of this explained to him and he has agreed to plead guilty. I don't know what he is doing now."

The judge turns to the translator and says that he will break the several charges down and ask how the accused pleads. He reads the first charge and asks again whether the accused is pleading guilty or not guilty. Again there is a translation, and a response in Inuktitut. Again the translator looks confused. She asks something in Inuktitut. The man replies with a long story. The translator says that the old man is telling her a story she does not understand. She cannot make sense of what he is saying. The defence lawyer, sighing, stands and says "Your honour, I have gone over this issue with my client. I would like to ask for a recess so that I can meet with my client one last time and explain the charges to him."

The judge pauses, then tells the lawyer to take his client out and talk with him again in the presence of a translator. The lawyer bows as he collects his files. The translator says something in Inuktitut to the man, who rises and follows the lawyer out of the room. The old Inuk woman gets up and goes after them.

While they are leaving, Louisa turns to me and says, "He doesn't understand what they are asking him. There is no word in Inuktitut for guilt. When she is translating the word, she is saying the word '*pasigatsa.*' That means 'are you the person that is to blame?'

When Louisa and I described the case involving the old man to the Inuit social-services workers the following week, they insisted that the old man knew what the word meant. He had been through this before and was manipulating the court with language. They advised us not to be taken in by him.

The clerk calls the next case by name of the accused. A defence lawyer at the legal-aid table rises quickly to his feet. He would like to ask that in this particular case the accused be able to remain in the audience and not come forward to the defence desk. "Why?" asks the judge. The lawyer responds that this will become obvious in the course of the proceedings. It is crucial for the defence that the accused remain anonymous during interrogation of the witnesses.

The judge hesitates, looks like he is thinking of saying something, then allows the motion. I notice that the two men who were reprimanded by the judge start to lean forward with interest.

The Crown prosecutor calls the first witness – who is one of the two men. As he places his coat on the chair before approaching the witness desk, he screens a smile at the other man, who smiles back.

The witness is asked if he needs a translator. He declines. The clerk asks him to raise his hand while putting one hand on the Bible and swearing to tell the truth. He does so. The Crown prosecutor asks him if he is Taamusi A. "Yes," he replies.

The Crown reads from a police statement, provided in February, five months prior to the court date. In the statement is the following account: The witness is the owner of a van. The owner has had his van taken on a number of occasions. The van has always been found the next day. On this occasion, in February, it was indeed found the next day on one of the roads close to town. It was undamaged, but the owner was tired of people taking his vehicle. He went on the FM radio band and offered a $50 reward to anyone who could tell him who had taken his van. The next day two young girls came to his house and told him they had seen Adami T. getting into the van. Taamusi A. went to the police and made a statement.

The Crown asks Taamusi A. if this was the statement that he provided the police. Taamusi A. indicates it is. The Crown says he has no further questions.

Kuujjuaq is completely inaccessible by road. Cars, pickup trucks, and vans arrive on the Ungava coast by ship over the short summer months. Beyond the town, there is one road that ends a couple of miles away at the dump. Another road leads for a few miles in the other direction to a lake. A third road going to the airport peters out past the airstrip in rolling rock tundra and scattered brush. Beyond the stump of each road are hundreds and hundreds of miles of wilderness. As one cannot not drive off anywhere with a car, people leave the keys in the ignition. There is nowhere to hide a stolen van in Kuujjuaq.

The legal-aid lawyer asks the witness to describe the van. He describes the make and colour. The lawyer asks him if his is the only van in Kuujjuaq. The owner replies that he is the only one who owns a van in Kuujjuaq. Is he sure? Yes, he is sure. The defence lawyer has no further questions.

The Crown calls the name of the next witness. She is not present so the clerk calls her name into the microphone.

The witness who enters is a pubescent Inuk girl. As she heads for the audience chairs, the Crown prosecutor makes a noise with his mouth to get her attention and directs her with his hand to the witness stand facing the judge. Her back is to us. She is thin. Her black hair is long and windblown with a narrow headband pulling it off her face. She has on a dirty pink windbreaker and pink sweat pants. As she stands facing the judge, I notice that her knees are double-jointed and point backwards. She stands taut with her hands in front of her, her knees pointing improbably towards us.

The judge asks if she needs a translator. The translator translates the question. The girl nods yes. The clerk asks her to put her hand on the Bible, raise her other hand and swear to tell the truth. There is a pause while this is translated. The girl does as asked. When she speaks, in Inuktitut, she is barely audible.

The Crown prosecutor reads from a second police statement which indicates that the girl saw the accused getting into the van. The prosecutor asks her if she made the statement. The translator translates. The girl says something, very softly, in Inuktitut. The translator indicates that she has not heard. The judge tells her to tell the girl to speak up and to move closer to the microphone. This is translated. The girl moves closer. The question is repeated. The girl, through the translator, says that that was what she told the police. (All of the following is through translation.)

The prosecutor asks the girl if the man she saw get into the van is in the room. The girl nods imperceptibly. The prosecutor asks her to say either yes or no. The girl says yes softly. He tells her to point to the man. She freezes.

He repeats the request that she point to the man. She keeps her body still and sweeps her arm in the direction of the audience. The prosecutor tells her to turn around and look at the man and point to him. As she

Kuujjuaq, being so small, is a place where the fourteen-year-old girl will with regular frequency have to run into the man at whom she pointed her finger.

turns quickly and finds the man with her eyes, points to him, and snaps back to her stiff position I see how stricken she looks.

The prosecutor grins and says he has no further questions. The girl has pointed to the man with whom the van owner has just been whispering, shaking hands, and exchanging smiles.

The legal-aid lawyer stands up. He asks the girl some questions about what she saw on the day that the van was taken, questions such as what side of the van she was on, who she was with, what time it was, what colour the van was. All of these questions are translated, and the girl makes muted replies. She is able to answer some of the questions, such as who she was with. To most of the rest she answers that she does not remember.

The defence lawyer repeats the questions to which the girl has replied she does not remember. The prosecutor starts to smirk. The defence continues his interrogation. After several minutes, the prosecutor rises, chuckling, and asks the judge to please ask the defence where he is going.

I notice at this point that the girl is crying. I can see her wiping her eyes and her voice, when it was audible, has been shaky.

The defence lawyer responds to the judge that he is building his case. The judge allows him to proceed.

The lawyer asks the girl more detailed questions about the event. The girl is visibly crying now. She says she does not remember. The Crown prosecutor continues to laugh, apparently at the legal-aid lawyer. The judge starts to smile as well as every question from the lawyer elicits the same translated answer. Louisa turns to me and whispers, "Why are they laughing?"

The questioning continues for several more minutes while the girl is crying, the Crown prosecutor chuckling, and the judge trying to hide a smile. At one point the clerk passes a glass of water to the girl.

Finally the judge tells the lawyer that the girl has given him an answer and that the questions are not going anywhere. The legal-aid lawyer insists to the judge that there are certain inconsistencies between the police statement and her testimony and that his client has a right to find those inconsistencies. The judge tells the lawyer to move on to another line of questioning.

The lawyer, who was beginning to hide a somewhat sheepish smile himself in response to the Crown prosecutor chuckling at every question, collects himself and changes his tack. He suggests that the only reason the girl came forward was because of the reward. He asks her if, indeed, this was not the case. The girl, sniffling, says she didn't want the money but Taamusi A. told her to take it. She says she heard Taamusi A. on the FM station asking if anyone had seen someone getting into his van, so she had gone to his house on her way home from school.

The legal-aid lawyer summarizes by suggesting that the girl only came forward because of the reward money. He has no further questions and, as this is a preliminary inquiry, he will be requesting that the witness appear again to testify. The girl stands at the witness desk. This is not translated for her. The judge tells her she can sit down in the audience chairs. This is translated and she turns, wiping her eyes, and walks to the chairs next to us. She sits as the next case is called, then gets up and leaves the room.

After a moment, I get up to follow her and see where she has gone. I want to see if she is all right. She is not in the hall when I go out. I see another girl standing in the hallway and ask her if she has seen where the first girl went. She went to the washroom with a friend. I go to the washroom but do not enter. I am not sure why Louisa did not come out with me. I am not sure what to do. I am not sure what I will say to the girl, apart from asking her if she is okay. After waiting outside the washroom for a few minutes, I go back to the courtroom.

In the courtroom, Simiunie C. is again standing, facing the judge. I sit down next to Louisa. The sentencing has resumed. The judge asks the defence lawyer if he has been able to find a case to support his claim that the judge should suspend sentencing pending outcome of an appeal. The lawyer rises, self-conscious, and says he has not. "No," says the judge, smiling. "I didn't think you would." He asks for further recommendations from the Crown and the defence.

The Crown offers nothing. The defence reiterates that the accused does not have a history of violence and that a community order would be more constructive for the accused while awaiting appeal. He sits down.

The judge begins by saying that this is the hardest case he has had to try in a long time. He has worked with the accused, who was a peace officer until this charge, for two years now and knows the accused has worked hard and done his job diligently in the community. He knows the accused is respected in the community. The charge of sexual assault, however, is a very serious one. The fact that the accused is a police officer does not make a difference in the sentencing. Because the charge is serious, he has to sentence appropriately. For that reason, he says, he is giving Simiunie C. a jail term of two years less a day to be served in Amos Correctional Centre. He attaches a variety of probation conditions to the jail term.

The judge passes some files to the clerk. The legal-aid lawyer writes something down, then rises and, bowing, leaves the room with Simiunie C.

The judge declares that there will be no more cases that evening. Court will resume the next day at 9 A.M. The clerk tells us to rise as the judge stands up, collects his files, and leaves the courtroom.

Once he is gone, Louisa and I turn to each other to talk. I tell her I am upset about what happened to the girl and concerned about her. Louisa is appalled at what happened. If the court wants to get respect from the Inuit by making them rise for the judge and remain silent in the audience, she says, then the court should respect the Inuit. She finds the way that the girl was treated to be disrespectful. She repeats that she could not believe that the judge was smiling and the Crown prosecutor laughing.

When we leave the courthouse, the young girl is at the entrance with another girl, standing between parked cars. Louisa knows them. The girl asks her something in Inuktitut. Louisa replies in Inuktitut. The girl and her friend say something else and leave. Louisa tells me the girl asked if she was allowed to leave the courthouse now. Louisa told her yes.

It is close to 11 P.M. now, and the sun has just gone down. The air is cold and the stars are starting to come out. Louisa offers to drive me home after she calls her brother to fetch her on his fourwheeler. I decline and tell her we will meet in the morning to discuss what we saw in court.

Introduction
Incorporating the Familiar

How much noticing could I permit myself without driving myself round the bend?
Too much noticing and I was too self-conscious to live; I trapped and paralyzed
myself, and dragged my friends down with me, so we couldn't meet each other's eyes,
my own loud awareness damning us both. Too little noticing, though – I would risk
much to avoid this – and I would miss the whole show. I would wake on my deathbed
and say, What was that?

Annie Dillard, An American Childhood

There was really nothing out of the ordinary about the chilly June circuit
of 1992. The participants, Inuit and Qallunaat, would probably be surprised to find that it had been noticed and singled out of the general flux
of history. The week had more banality than intrigue. What could it
contain that might sustain prolonged analysis?

Several tales could be scooped from that graceless collision of
moments in the basement of Kuujjuaq's old hospital. One could rum-
mage for the recommendations, which fairly jump out – recommendations that have crowded commissioned reports from the Marshall
Inquiry to the Inuit Justice Task Force. One could, as I did, run after the
girl to see if she's all right, or discuss with Louisa what we saw in court.
Here, though, I want to do something else.

I want to do what I in fact had to do in order to write up the event.
I could not incorporate it while it was still under my skin. I needed to
depart from the courthouse, the fluorescent lights, the blowing sand in
my ears and eyebrows, the near-incessant whine of fourwheelers.

I want to remove myself from the account of 1992 in order to make
strange that which is indeed common: the regular moments in which
humans struggle, with varying degrees of seemliness, to incorporate the
distinctive and unfamiliar into that which is familiar. But what is familiar to us is also what is distinctive about us – the things that a foreign
anthropologist or a novelist would settle upon. Grasping this oddness
through the ethnographic encounter is like beholding simultaneously
the contents and limits of the field of vision. One begins to see why in
anthropology so much emphasis has been placed on the otherness of the
other and so little on the shared realm where the similar and dissimilar
meet. The tone of our encounters is so close to the bone that on our

deathbed we might reflect with surprise that it has made up our lives. It was not only *their* lives that were being lived in the field.

But we cannot write from our deathbed, unless we stretch out the moment so it no longer has any meaning. We can only write "as if": as if we could grasp the whole, as if we could grasp also this moment's grasp.

This is also the problem with ethnography. Ethnographers are attuned to the effort of being neither too self-conscious to be in the moment nor too in the moment to appreciate it. Beyond this struggle, they only notice with difficulty that the moment stands out from a commonplace field which is second nature to them. Failing to force *that* field into the mind, they overlook the background on which the other and the self are exposed. They also risk missing the human import of their inquiry.

Out of the taken-for-granted background that propped up the June circuit, I want to focus on three zones where the familiar and the unfamiliar merge: a sense of reality, a sense of self, and a sense of injustice. The three main chapters of this book, then, will deal with the incorporation of the other's sense of reality into history, the other's sense of self into intimacy, and the other's sense of injustice into law.

This may seem like an unusually ample scope for a book that is ostensibly an investigation into the accommodation between Aboriginal and non-Aboriginal legal systems. This amplitude derives from the conviction that a study of conflict between legal systems is really more about conflict of underlying sensibilities, each subtly informed by alternative cultural codes. It is not helpful to understand any single feature of a legal system without seeing its connectedness with other features and without locating it within a complex social, multicultural, and historical context.

In this manner, the text should work in two directions. Exploring the quandaries of intercultural communication and judgment should help us to understand what viable legal pluralism might look like. Conversely, contemplating how diverse senses of injustice might be mutually recognized should evoke an instance of the possibilities for a humane society. If this is a book about law, it is also a book about how understanding law can illuminate the sense we make of a human life, and vice versa.

The text, then, attempts to illuminate the underlying multiplicity and specificity of understandings that give coherence to concepts of law. The particularity of these understandings is an important part of why different legal sensibilities would not be easily codified and thus rendered commensurable with one another. The rootedness of a sense of injustice in a concrete historical consciousness precludes such a neutral distillation from the various expressions of legal sensibility. The essence of a particular injustice is, to a very large extent, the concrete details of which it is composed.

I want to avoid, however, a simple taxonomy of difference. The text is not meant to be only descriptive. It intends to get at overall similarities and relationships between phenomena, to explore the possibilities for generalizations and shared meanings. Just as attention to particulars critically informs a sense of injustice, attention to the sense made of injustice concentrates the ability to imagine and describe particulars – to notice.

The argument of the book thus negotiates around two dangerous tendencies in discussions about social and legal accommodation. The first is a tendency to subsume particular events and configurations into a general rule, to move too quickly from the enigmatic complexities of circumstances to a simplified and putatively neutral version of reality. The second tendency places too great insistence on the relativity of understanding, refusing to generalize in deference to manifest cultural difference. Both of these tendencies preclude the richness of possibilities for communication. Neither, I will argue, reflects the ways in which dialogue about accommodation actually proceeds.

This way of thinking about legal and social diversity cannot be adequately stated in the language of conventional legal theory or exposition. As Martha Nussbaum notes, "any style makes, itself, a statement ... an abstract theoretical style makes, like any other style, a statement about what is important and what is not, about what faculties of the reader are important for knowing and what are not."[1] I would argue that discerning abilities in reading legislation and case law are not the only faculties that are required in the study of and writing about law; this is particularly so when the subject of investigation deals with non-legislated, non-textual, non-state legal orders. Some of the understandings I am attempting to convey require a literary style more attuned to the diversity and situatedness of experience.

But the argument presented in the text also demonstrates a commitment to reach for similarities and common ground. This requires, again, a different stylistic refinement. Both of these commitments are reflected in the overall literary structure of the work. The manuscript is divided into three distinct sections. Each section contains two writing styles, one concrete and particular, the other abstract and theoretical. The narrative account that precedes each theoretical excursion not only sets up a dilemma but also serves to ground the following discussion. The reflective style that follows each narrative account reveals the importance of reaching for relevance. The reader is thus invited to move imaginatively back and forth, checking general against particular truths, adding to the text his or her own situated understanding.

The three sections follow an argument whose progress reflects the kind of dialogic manner in which the negotiation of intercultural law proceeds. Evidence of structural clarity in the argument is belied, to some extent, by the very often messy and contested nature of the content.

The first narrative, "Circuit Court/Circus Court," is an ethnographic account of the itinerant court in Kuujjuaq culled from fieldwork carried out in the summer of 1992. It sets up the problems of the delivery of justice amongst Inuit communities and evokes the cultural determinacy of understanding. The attendant theoretical chapter, "Toponymy and Its Objects," picks up and elaborates on the theme of cross-cultural tension and miscommunication suggested by the events of that evening of 18 June 1992 emphasizing the ways in which distinctive Inuit and Qallunaat histories have shaped understanding.

In exploring the histories of Nunavik I focus on the habits that history has inculcated, its unsensed imprint incorporated in us. This common sense confirms for us the limits of the natural world. And this natural world is the bedrock on which spades turn in attempts to ground the legitimacy of justice. What more can be said to convince one who is not compelled? Ask anybody, we say, confident ... desperate. Everybody knows.

The second narrative section, "The Children under the Bed," also derives from the fieldwork period of 1992. Just as one of the central themes of the book is the ways in which legal systems deal with the problem of family violence, the principle focus of attention in the field was on local experiences of such violation. People from Kuujjuaq shared their often deeply troubling accounts of what they had lived through. These stories were collected, transcribed, and, while safeguarding the anonymity of the narrators, redistributed to the community in the form of a booklet. This section presents two of those stories. It suggests an antithesis to the first narrative/theoretical pair, namely that cultures are constituted by different and often contending sets of experiences.

This theme is developed from a theoretical standpoint in "Lovers and Healing Circles." In elaborating the divergences and overlaps of group-specific experience, the chapter works through how belonging shapes understanding and identity. The issue is explored by an investigation into the grammar of identity and intimacy. Against the common sense of history, we play out our love lives. The public language of intimacy shapes our private moments, conveying what is appropriate and what is not, humanizing desire. It does so in ways that alienate us miserably or confirm our sense of being at home in our skins. This chapter also focuses on the ways in which agency is qualified by force and the nature of the recovery required to restore an abject identity, the nature of the attention required to attend to another human being.

The third narrative, "Circuit/Circus/Circle," suggests an awkward synthesis on the ground of the various dilemmas raised in the first two sections. It is an ethnographic account of Nunavik's first sentencing circle – a family violence case heard in the spring of 1993. The attendant theoretical section, "Agents of Justice/Agents of Love," is also a synthesis which tries to accommodate the several dilemmas into a tentative approach to the material. In examining concerns about the determinacy of rules in law, I employ a Wittgensteinian analysis to underline how shared practices and dispositions lend coherency and warrant to legal propositions. I argue that juridical rules emerge from the recognized values in which the group feels at home. Locating the coherence of legal systems in the shared backgrounds of participants suggests ways of rendering the taken-for-granted culture of law unfamiliar and hence more open to judgment, more responsive to unfamiliar perspectives. The injustices of exclusion from the official community of Everybody and Anybody is the legal theme that courses through this text.

In all of the confrontations of the familiar and the unfamiliar set out in the following material, there is no claim to a truth beyond the common, ordinary, historical world into which we were born, no language unendowed with an accent in which to utter it. It is only with others – if only through the acquisition of language – that we acquire a sense of being present and at home in the world. Justice, conceivably, is the attempt to perceive the spectacular arbitrariness of the familiar, to struggle for that lonely distance from all things that are so intimately ours that we consider them as ourselves, a struggle that allows us to see the other, homeless and transient as ourselves.

This book is a one-off of those struggles.

Toponymy and Its Objects

It is significant that "culture" is sometimes described as a *map;* it is the analogy which occurs to an outsider who has to find his way around in a foreign landscape and who compensates for his lack of practical mastery, the prerogative of the native, by the use of a model of all possible routes. The gulf between this potential, abstract space, devoid of landmarks or any privileged centre ... and the practical space of journeys actually made, or rather of journeys actually being made, can be seen from the difficulty we have in recognizing familiar routes on a map or town-plan until we are able to bring together the axes of the field of potentialities and the "system of axes linked unalterably to our bodies, and carried about with us wherever we go", as Poincaré puts it, which structures practical space into right and left, up and down, in front and behind.

Pierre Bourdieu, *Outline of a Theory of Practice*[1]

It is common for books on the Eastern Arctic to have at least one map of the area under discussion. The readers of these maps fill in implied points of reference with their stock of geographical knowledge. They locate landmarks, indulge the simple pleasure of recognition, scan unfamiliar contours and names, bring their topographical uncertainties into line. In clarifying uncertainties, they do not question the accuracy of the map. It is taken to be a reliable representation of the object. It is not the focus of the text.

The boundaries of these maps conventionally contain, at the outer margins or in a zoom, a frontier between inside and outside. The map is the realm where the two meet. These lines do not form a natural boundary. They are framed by the map. A map with a different purpose would emphasize other horizons, other relations between things. Maps arbitrarily contain an aspect of the world.

For the purpose it sets out to fulfil, however, a map is transparent: the world's peculiar nature looms up through it. More scrupulous attention to an area brings prior maps, devoted to the same inquiry, into line. The refined map becomes the standard against which other maps are checked. Here, emphasis on the map's artificiality is irrelevant, even pedantic.

Ethnography is to culture what maps are to landscape. It posits a border from the frontiers of which the ethnographer reports home. But the boundaries of culture are neither fixed nor absolute. The practice that collects the wild disparity of individual experience into durable groupings fails to collect that equally predictable disparity. Nonetheless, in the field of ethnography, statements about the probable experiences of the group's members are more or less improbable.

History, similarly, cuts a path through the past with its plot. And the same tension between representation and reality marks texts that place maps, culture, and history in the same frame. Although they toy with the sincerity of representations, if they are (as they aspire to be) artfully and faithfully rendered, the world comes more clearly into view.

The following is a map of how one might reach the starting point of an Arctic week in June 1992 along the 68th longitude west. The court was operating with a sense of propriety that, from the point of view of an outsider to its culture, might seem almost boorish. The following material is an investigation into the historical antecedents of both that sense of propriety and the points of view from which the events appear jarring. Before coming back to a history of the circuit court and the tensions between it and Inuit communities in Nunavik, the text takes a long route through some of the cultural histories, separate and shared, that normalize both the court and our responses to it. It lays out some of the divergent system of axes linked unalterably to the bodies of those who entered the courtroom on that evening.

Just as the subtext to the preceding text cast the narrative in different light, and just as the perspective from the court's audience contrasts with the point of view of those parading in front of it, the following material intends to illuminate our immediate response to that evening from an historical point of view.

NUNAVIK

In 1988, ACI [Avataq Cultural Institute] took an additional step and requested of the Commission de Toponymie du Québec (CTQ) the acceptance of Nunavik as a regional name for the Inuit homeland in northern Québec ... Nunavik is the contiguous land and sea area occupied and used by the Inuit who, today, live in permanent and temporary settlements along the coastline of mainland Nunavik. The limits of Nunavik represent the outer geographical reach of those areas and places which the Inuit have named and used. Thus, as a region, Nunavik represents the Inuit homeland based on continual land use and occupancy and on the congruous and contiguous naming of places and spaces throughout the area.

L. Müller-Wille, *Place Names, Territoriality and Sovereignty*[2]

Nunavik is a recent construct. It could not be found, prior to 1988, on any Qallunaat map that covered the land. Moreover, it is new to the Inuit. Once the Inuit Place Names Project had collected, transcribed, and organized Inuit place names for the area, the Inuit realized they did not have a name for the entity as a whole.[3] They settled on Nunavik.

The entity, however, is a collage of perspectives, many borrowed from the outside. These include aerial and naval viewpoints, the understanding of cultures, peoples, and nations as bounded entities, and anthropological assumptions about where a people begin and end. Nunavik is thoroughly infused with realities originally outside of (and now inside) its boundaries. As an intercultural object, it no more represents the way the original Inuit saw the land than a glass-bottomed boat reveals the perspective of the fish being observed.

Nunavik is the historical outcome of contact with Qallunaat. Its sophistication comes from its strategic manipulation of Inuit identity, consolidating its content internally while defending an Inuit territory against the encroachment of outsiders. The central use of Nunavik is political. Nunavik is distinctively Inuit; but it is also shrewdly Inuit.

The political aspirations of Nunavik can be seen in the project's methodology. The scope of traditional land use was layered into the collective memory of Inuit elders by habitual return and by a mnemonic retracing of those tracks, both with and for other Inuit. The project transcribed this embodied knowledge into "written, standardized and politically accepted information."[4] These standards and political requirements were not set by the Inuit but rather appropriated by them, ready-made. The cultural resource of place names was collected both with and for non-Inuit.

This selection of cohorts is pragmatic. As Müller-Wille notes, "Any contemporary toponymic study, if it is to result in official approval and legal status, now has to be conducted within the legal constraints concerning place names in a political territory."[5] By keeping apace with official topography, the Inuit secured their place on the political map.

A judge might, as the next circuit takes flight, pragmatically ask for a map of his or her new jurisdiction and do little more than check which places have been renamed what. This gloss would miss much of the richness – and subversiveness – of Nunavik. The contours of the new political entity give rise to questions of legitimacy in the delivery of law in the area. They quietly draw attention to some of the artificiality of the official order.

Although Nunavik exploits Qallunaat orthodoxies, it is not contained by them. The court's jurisdiction, for example, coincides with an earlier entity. After the James Bay Agreement in 1976 and until the Nunavik name change, this region was called, for administrative purposes, the Kativik Region. For electoral purposes, it was Nouveau-Québec. Neither designator represents fully the area used by the Inuit of the communities along the coast of northern Québec. The boundaries of the Kativik/Nouveau-Québec jurisdictions end mainly in the offshore area at the tidal low-water line between the Northwest Territories and Québec. According to Inuit spatial perception, these lines do not exist.

These lines do not reflect the four-dimensional seasonal expansion and dilation of the ice floe that Nunavik incorporates into its whole. Nunavik represents the continuous Inuit place-name system that embraces both the coast and the off-shore region, a territory consisting of land, water, and ice as a spatial network.

Inuit place names do more than render a previously fixed boundary more fluid and seasonally dependent. The network that makes up the Inuit place-name system is based not only on human-land relations but on relations between species. The flux of the limits of Inuit territory is dependent on a subtle and intricate interweaving of humans and animals over the land and ice and under the water.

This interlacing of species pervades Inuit understanding of the habits, relationships, and movements of animals. The patterns of land use that have evolved in the region are rooted in this understanding. Even the two-dimensional place-name maps are doubly notional for failing to capture the temporal shifts in ice floes and this overlapping movement of species. Lines drawn on maps might offer a summary of land use per species hunted, but the lines represent neither a natural frontier nor the outer limit to which animals are pursued. In the case of the white fox, which has a four-year population cycle, the lines may change quadrannually; in the case of the beluga whale, which has been decimated in Arctic waters, the lines may change for generations.

The relation between this order of spatial perception and the court may not be immediately apparent. The implications, however, are not far from the surface. On whose territory, for example, is a crime committed if it happens on the ice over the sea of Nunavik and not the ice over the land? This obscure hypothetical evokes Michel Brochu, the Québécois cartographer, concerned about administrative sovereignty over Nouveau-Québec in the 1960s. As he noted about the low-water line frontier:

Les conséquences de ces limites absurdes peuvent se faire sentir jusque dans le domaine policier: en effet, des Esquimaux ayant commis un délit ou un crime, justiciables devant les tribunaux du Québec, pourraient échapper à la police du Québec simplement en se réfugiant sur une île à quelques centaines de mètres de la rive. Il faudrait alors, soit que le Québec demande à Ottawa l'autorisation de poursuivre un individu passible d'arrestation, soit encore que la Police Montée de Frobisher, ou de Cap Dorset se déplace sur des distances considérables et vienne arrêter les prévenus qu'elle déférera au parquet de Québec.[6]

Shifting borders strain an already troublesome struggle for control of the territory.

The added stress, however, demands more than simply nailing down the slippery lines or even coordinating the scope of police itineraries with the seasons. Nunavik, as a homeland entity, conjures up new and perturbing questions of authority. If the Inuit perception of space is officialized, then why not distinctively Inuit versions of history and law? This validation could leave the court's jurisdiction on rather shaky ground. The question of whose police pursue whom onto whose territory becomes more complex, and more redundant. The very legitimacy of these institutions – police, court, territory – is undermined.

The implications for history and law are intimated by the project itself. In order to translate the four-dimensional space of the Inuit onto a two-dimensional plane, the cartographers had to make contact with the elaborate coherencies of that world. This sensibility shines through the synoptic apprehension of the maps. Buoying up the practice of naming is a whole way of ordering reality, of ordering social and natural relations, of ordering historical events. Place names relate to each other for description and orientation. They constitute a system. As a syntax encoding spatial behaviour, place names "enable hunters to construct oral maps by which they can visualize areas, approximate distances, and recognize travel routes."[7] They orient those familiar with a practice but uncertain about all of its possibilities.

Place names also constitute a descriptive record of the landscape. Qallunaat give the name Helicopter Island to the island where a helicopter landed in 1953 and Cape Bernard Shaw to a contour resembling, from the air, the profile of George Bernard Shaw. The Inuit give the name Tiluq to the place where two men exchanged blows over some eggs, the name Niguklik (meaning a slimy place) to the site where people used to fish for cod and their hands would get slimy from working with them, the name Tasiujalugasak (meaning it looks like a pond that nobody likes) to a salt-water pond.[8] These descriptions mark a world of distinctive values and practices.

Place names thus constitute a record of how the Inuit organized space and identified its particular assets. As a record, they are a form of history. As Hugh Brody noted in 1977 about Labrador Inuit land use, "The language of story telling and the naming of places convey the depth of Inuit tradition in Labrador. Places named in stories and myths are still places on the ground, and places on the ground are links to Inuit past through the events, both real and fantastic, that are said to have occurred there. Events from the undated and undatable past of myths unite the modern life of Inuit of today with the traditional life of more than two centuries ago."[9] Place names are, for the Inuit, a way of speaking about who they were and who they are.

Place names also attest to the appropriation of space into the environmental perception of the Inuit. As a system of spatial integration, they represent aspects of territorial control. And this is one criterion for determining where a people rightfully begin and end.

This connection between naming and dominion has indeed been exploited to legally ground Inuit attempts to carve a sphere of autonomy out of the modern state. Legal arguments have been successfully advanced to counter the notion that the Inuit, lacking an analogue to private ownership, inhabited a legal void.[10] Lawyers, staking a territorial claim on behalf of the Inuit, place emphasis on the presence of a *system* of land use and occupancy. This system makes up a local legal order which is, in theory, knowable to lawyers who produce it as evidence in court to delimit the boundaries between Inuit and non-Inuit jurisdictions.

The Inuit are not the only ones, however, to exploit the political significance of names.

INUKSUIT AND THE CONTINGENCY OF MAPS

Inuksuit:
Plural for *inuksuk*, which means "to act in the capacity of a human."
a) a person-like thing
b) a special stone object or figure constructed by a person in a variety of ways
   so as to:
   – assist in hunting
   – serve as a message, sign, or signal
   – function as an indicator, locator, marker, or co-ordination point
   – serve as a symbol

- act as a memorial
- be an object of power or veneration
- have a purpose known only to its builder
- have astronomical significance

Nick Hallendy, "The Last Known Traditional Inuit Trial..."[11]

Part of the Qallunaat compulsion to name places and draw up maps is a need, very similar to that of the Inuit, to fix who they are and how they relate to the land and to each other. Maps are historical and cultural artifacts. If Qallunaat needs were so modest, however, it would not be incumbent on the Inuit to frame their geographical history in terms opposable to territorial encroachment. While there is a jurisdictional connection between maps and the quality of the presence of the itinerant court in Nunavik, this connection is also historical. Maps and naming, as it turns out, lay out a moral jurisdiction for the law, based on a particular view of history.

The land captured by "Nunavik" has been the object of several historical disputes about maps. The political dimension of place names was invoked in the North as recently as 1962 by Brochu, the Québec cartographer.[12] While Québec had underlying title to the territory since the 1912 *Québec Boundary Extension Act,* it did not administratively occupy the territory until the 1960s. The federal government provided basic services to the Inuit, including education, social services, policing, and health care. To signal the political presence of the province on the territory, Brochu suggested, in conjunction with administrative replacement, an overhaul of the region's place names. Until then official maps were dominated by titles such as Wakeham Bay, Cape Wolstenholme, and Port Harrison. In 1961 the provincial minister of Lands and Forests announced the official adoption by the Comité de Toponomie du Québec of a new list of French names for the territory of Nouveau-Québec. As Brochu noted, "cette politique symbolise la détermination bien arrêtée de la province de Québec de marquer sa présense française dans ces régions nouvelles."[13] Symbolic appropriation of a territory is a critical index of control.

The use of place names as a "message, sign, or signal" of dominion has a deeper history than the Commission de Toponomie du Québec. Nunavik was a site of the struggles between the French and British crowns over, among other things, maps. Toponymic dispute was a component of a larger disagreement about the criteria for acquiring sovereignty over the recently "discovered" lands of North America. One argument ran that sovereignty could be perfected by a series of gestures or demonstrations intending to encompass a swathe of land within the ritual. Such actions included the performance of ceremonies on the beachhead, the unfurling of the sovereign or a national standard, the recital of various ritual legal or religious formulae, or the erection of a stone cairn or a wooden cross. The rival side pointed out the self-serving nature of these devices, claiming that greater energy was required to take *effective* possession of a territory. The disagreement over the legal status of such rituals is echoed in the seventeenth-century dispute between Britain and France over the Eastern Arctic.[14]

The British claimed title to all of Hudson's Bay and its hinterland, shored up by the symbolic acts of possession performed by a chain of British explorers from Cabot to Hudson. In 1670 Charles II granted a colonial charter to the Hudson's Bay Company over this land, giving it a monopoly over the fur trade in the region and empowering it to exclude every European outsider from the Bay. The French responded by attacking the company's post at Fort Nelson in 1682, thereby triggering a series of diplomatic exchanges between the British and French to determine, between themselves, who had valid title.

When Britain pointed to their explorers' trail of gestures, France retorted that such rituals were empty and insisted that "Tis well knowne that Collony's cannot bee wholly established but by time & the Care & paines of those who have the managemt. of it."[15] The British, recognizing that they could not possibly have had effective control of the whole of Hudson Bay, relied instead on the fact that "All the Rivers Lakes Streights Islands Capes and Promontoryes are called by English names and are soe denominated even in Sanson's Mapps which hee lately dedicated to the Dauphin ... The names which [the maps] Generally give to Country's are Conveinceing marks of the Propriety."[16] A web of English names had been spread out over representations of the land, and this was testimony to the care and pains required to capture the whole within British title.

The French rejoinder to the invocation of maps (even those dedicated to the future king of France) sets up nicely the general quandaries of map-making. French diplomats responded that "[i]f one would admitt these sorts of Profes the French will make appeare by Divers priviledged Relations printed at London, that all the Country's in Question, did belong to them before the English knew them, and this alone would end the Contest."[17] In this manner, anyone, by the simple act of transcribing names onto a page, could thereby claim title. Thus degenerates the entire quest for legitimacy.

Further, a suspicion is raised about the general accuracy of maps. From Sanson's to Nunavik's, the affiliation of the maps of the area with territorial aspirations suggests that their contours are shaped by particular interests and are therefore somewhat arbitrary. This connection also intimates a difficulty in grasping a real object against which to check self-serving representations.

The complexities of cartography, as we have seen, are not irrelevant for determining legal jurisdiction. Neither are they irrelevant for historiography, as we will see: the historian needs to locate herself. But when Robin Collingwood noted that one of the distinctions between novels and history is that "everything in [history] must stand in some relation to everything else, even if that relation is only topographical and chronological," he must have envisaged a world where topographical names stood for one thing and did not shift with the seasons or depend on the direction of approach.[18]

In the face of the apparent contingency of maps, it is tempting to overlook the ways that, between people, maps are often held to be meaningful representations. This can be seen even in the different manner in which the various maps of the region were received. The quality of response suggests that standardization *is* possible and that historiography (as well as law), though often interested, might be grounded in more than rhetoric.

The British were grasping with their toponymic claims, and the French suitably derisive in their response. Some version of this characterization would likely have been conceded by both sides, if only subliminally in the readiness of France's response and Britain's ultimate recourse to other justifications and claims to possession. Brochu's linguistic challenge to the legitimacy of "Northern Quebec" was politic and timely, as the federal government's retreat confirms. And someone who challenges the toponym "Nunavik" is either unaware of the 1988 name change, unaware of its official status, or quite possibly chauvinistic. He or she would stand alone, or at least on the fringes of respectable cartography. Between people, some maps are taken for granted and others are subject to scrutiny.

The relation between map-making and sovereignty illustrates the simultaneously arbitrary and meaningful nature of practices. If there had been the same agreement between the British and French that place naming gave title as there was to the idea that discovery had to be accompanied by at least *some* form of possession, then the matter would have been settled by Sanson's Mapps. As names were not jointly accepted as sufficient proof, their relevance was contested in a volley of diplomatic exchanges. But these very arguments about naming only made sense in the context of a shared tradition of acquiring territory beyond one's realm and determining acquisition by the conventions of discovery and possession. These activities assume *some* stability in cartographic conventions. The diplomatic exchanges could only get off the ground if some things were not matters for discussion.

The same emphasis on the common ground of disputes can be drawn in the postcolonial context in which the Inuit and Qallunaat negotiate the official contours of the northern world. While it might seem, from the arbitrariness of conventions, that communication across conventional orders is near-impossible, there is a stable background of graceful exchange between peoples against which awkwardness stands out as unseemly and draws attention to itself. Out of, and perhaps as a result of, the dogmatic arguments of imperial powers, a custom has emerged of naming certain gestures and acts as ethnocentric and self-serving – a custom that is developing the same kind of normality that the conjunction of discovery and possession had between the British and French in their assertions of sovereignty. This is the environment in which the distinct outlines of Nunavik have taken shape. It is also the context in which the court's second nature is scrutinized.

The shifting normality from the imperial to the postcolonial context indicates that some concepts stand still while discussions and disagreements spin around them and hold them in place. But these axes are not absolutely attached to "reality"; they can shift and are then held in place by other conventional agreements. Collingwood has made this point with respect to the factual world of history: "All that the historian means, when he describes certain historical facts as his data, is that for the purpose of a particular piece of work there are certain historical problems relevant to that work which for the present he proposes to treat as settled; though, if they are settled, it is only because historical thinking has settled them in the past, and they remain settled only until he or someone else decides to reopen them." [19] Although the propositions that are presupposed by the traffic of our ordinary behaviour are stable, they are not fixed.

The reopening of things that have been treated as settled can be compared to the principle of judicial notice in law. The rules of evidence and procedure in law determine what things are considered relevant for proof and how those things are to be proven. But they do not prove every fact on the legal landscape, nor are there rules of exclusion for every conceivable irrelevance. Indeed, the ability of the rules to function is predicated on some things being the background for which the tableau of proofs is foreground. So, for example, it is not ordinarily part of a lawyer's job to prove that the court is in Canada and that the laws of Canada are authoritative. The court takes judicial notice of these "facts." But there are limiting cases that might call into question this common sense. And those things of which the court takes judicial notice may determine the outcome of a case.[20]

One of the things the itinerant court took judicial notice of in the June circuit of 1992 was that its operations were a legitimate act of authority. The lawyers did not need to prove that the relevant law was Qallunaat with its rules of evidence and procedure. They did not need to begin by proving they were on Qallunaat territory. They did not need to establish the appropriateness of their very purpose and presence.

But this sense of propriety is called into question by the geographical entity Nunavik and by its corresponding history. Nunavik, the place name, gives judicial notice to a contending etiquette that contests not merely the necessity of earlier maps but the very normality of political control over a foreign realm, a normality that made sense of both seventeenth-century imperial diplomacy and a good part of Qallunaat map-making.

The bluster of dominion might be illustrated with a pile of rocks that is currently stacked in downtown Montréal. In the South, non-aesthetic objects from other cultures may be transformed into art objects by locating them within an aesthetic gaze. In this manner, an inuksuk was commissioned for a spot on Sherbrooke Street directly across from McGill University. For those who commissioned it and for those who pass it by every day, the inuksuk has a sturdy presence, though an innocuous one from the point of view of political authority. Our aesthetic and legal conventions make it unnecessary to add that this pile of rocks bears no analogy to the rock cairns that contributed to the arsenal of sovereignty in the imperial era. It goes without saying that the inuksuk is not an historical monument to evolving and expanding Inuit notions of spatial appropriation.

If the Inuk "artist" agreed that between the Inuit and us the object was purely aesthetic, but now told us that between the Inuit and Naskapi it indicated which of them could build rock piles in Montréal, we would find this odd, not particularly troubling, only inconvenient when we desire a Naskapi pile of rocks. For the most part, this would be an internal dispute between two remote peoples. Let them argue things out between themselves, we would say, we have our art object.

But if the Inuk claimed that the building of inuksuit has always served as a way of marking the limits of Inuit territory, that Montréal was now within Inuit territory, that its resources were now part of the Inuit patrimony, and that the very commission of an inuksuk was evidence of acquiescence, we would be taken aback by the impropriety of such a claim. If the Inuit could back up this claim with an irresistible force, we would, without doubt, protest. We would insist that there was no agreement for this interpretation. We would be defiant even if the Inuit did not listen to us and we were overpowered by them.

In the postcolonial context, however, we can feel fortified in our indignation that the silence of one party in the face of the other's might does not constitute agreement. There is some recognition that measurement by the same standard requires the harmonization of incongruous frames of reference. And outside of this imaginary exercise, this standardization is occurring. In order that such an accord might be reached in Nunavik, the Inuit conceded the language of inuksuit and four-dimensional spatial perception for the language of maps and territory. But with its concession, it invited the court to take judicial notice of more than its superficial toponymy. It invited the court to read through the thin surface of the maps into the layers of depth keeping it in cartographic place. A significant part of this depth is historical.

NUNA

[The Eskimos] are a fragmented, amorphous race that lacks all sense of history, inherits no pride of ancestry, and discerns no glory in past events or past achievements. Until we Europeans shattered their isolation four centuries ago they were more rigidly confined than the dwellers in Plato's cave: no shadowy figures from the outer world ever flickered on their prison wall to provoke new images and new ideas, and not even a Mohammed could have drawn them out of that prison to unite them into a nation.

Diamond Jenness, *Eskimo Administration*[21]

Nunavik challenges the Qallunaat sense of place. But it does so on the non-Inuit turf of the Commission de Toponymie du Québec. Approaching Nunavik's pre-standardized frame of reference requires, among other things, illuminating Diamond Jenness's shadowy assumptions about history which enabled him to fill in the Inuit sense of history with a void. These blind suppositions come more clearly into the light when provoked by contrasting Inuit understandings of history. The physical setting of this latter history would not have been identical to Nunavik.

To locate this history, I have selected the unofficial toponym "Nuna," which is the word for "land" in the Inupik and Upik dialects. Nuna suggests the more inclusive sense of "country." It is the territory "within which a man lives out his life [and] is possessed by him."[22] It is far from the spatial object of conventional history, giving rise to as many questions as it does answers. Where does the "country" begin, and where does it end? Is the extent of the country determined by the extent to which one spreads oneself out over the land? Does it shift with shifts in usage? And what is the Inuit counterpart to being "possessed by"?

Despite its problems as a referent, the relative opacity of the term signals that this approach to history is not searching for fixed objects. It is searching to orient itself towards an Inuit historical consciousness by a preliminary reorientation away from predominantly southern conceptions of territory and land.

Nuna also disguises a telescoping series of historical interactions. Although the word may have existed prior to European contact, it has been shaped, analogously with Nunavik, by contact with *other* others like the Dorset Inuit, the Cree and Naskapi, or indeed other *miut* groups than the speakers of Inupik and Upik.[23]

The Inuit bracketed by Nuna might have seen themselves as part of a people that overspilled the boundaries of Nunavik. The border between the Northwest Territories and Québec, for example, is artificial for the Inuit, kin being spread over the two territories. The frontier with Labrador is similarly contrived. Furthermore, the circuit court's jurisdiction may include groups of Inuit who did not always see themselves as part of one people. The Nunavik region, for example, towards the late nineteenth century, embraced three regional *miut* groups: the Siqinirmiut, the Tarramiut, and the Itivimiut.[24] Indeed the court's ambit may include not only distinct groups but people with a history of conflict. Hence the Thule Inuit are said to have replaced the Dorset Inuit by the fourteenth century in the circumpolar region of Canada by exterminating or replacing them through warfare, expropriation of hunting territory, or amalgamation.[25] The "Inuit of Quebec" do not exist as an entity outside of things like welfare disbursements, legal jurisdictions, and land-claim settlements. A history of Nuna would spill over the spatial confines of Nunavik.

There are other elements in standard historiography that might restrict an Inuit historical imagination: the very definition of inuksuit alludes to one. An inuksuk is a "person-like thing." This definition seems straightforward. We understand the term "person." We feel we can easily picture a thing that resembles a person. If the Qallunaat concept of space is not exactly congruent with the Inuit, the category of the person seems to provide a common handle.

The category of the person is not of secondary importance to historical accounts: the person is the subject of historical accounts. For Qallunaat, this means, for example, that if you want to describe the movement, over time, of animals on the land, you would not be doing generic history. And a history of the people in the region following European contact would make at least obtuse reference to their activities. Europeans are, in a sense that is so obvious as to make the statement meaningless, persons.

But the idea of the person is neither universal nor immutable. It is a concept that is embedded in a social context. As Marcel Mauss notes, "It is formulated only for us, among us."[26] Indeed, there is not a strict equivalence between the Inuit and Qallunaat category of the person. For Qallunaat, the idea of the person is roughly coordinate with the legal category of the person, an autonomous human being, equal to other autonomous units, the titulary of rights and obligations. The very word "Inuit," meaning "human beings," suggests an incongruence with this understanding, as does the self-referent "*Inutuinnait*" which means "true human beings."[27] The Inuit did not share an inability to question the personhood of Europeans. Nor would the Inuit have overlooked the personhood of animals.

Evidence for the Inuit concept of the person surfaces in anthropological accounts. Edward Adamson Hoebel noted, for example, the multiplicity of taboos that revolved around animals, most of them "directed to spirits of animals or their controlling deities in order to guard against conduct offensive or disrespectful to them."[28] Each species had an archetypal soul (*turnqaniq*), and the souls were revered and surrounded by taboos. Violation of a taboo had serious consequences as angered animals would shun the local territory, thereby threatening the community with starvation. An infraction could lead to the banishment of the offender from the community, even in the dead of winter.

Animals also had individual souls which were surrounded with taboos. Thus there were taboos about the proper methods of hunting animals. If they were respected, the soul of the dead animal would re-enter a new one, which could then be pursued by the hunter in the future. If they were ignored, the soul "remained free-floating in the cosmos without influence upon the people; these animal souls would not join a new animal and thus there would be no game."[29]

There is also evidence for the attribution of personhood to animals in naming practices. For the Inuit, human beings had two souls which gave an individual strength and personality – a human soul and a name soul. The human soul was "unique to each person and accounted for the individuality of the Inuk."[30] The name soul floated freely about the cosmos; it was "not only within the body of the Inuk but also invisibly about him or her." Although the name soul was particularized in an individual, the individual shared its atemporal aspects with others of the same name. Children were expected to have characteristics in common with others of their name. With the death of an individual, the name soul would become detached and float about freely until called upon at a naming ritual to enter a new child. The naming ritual could also call upon the name to enter the body of an animal.[31]

Society, then, was not just made up of human beings. It was composed of human and non-human members, and human persons were not superior to non-human persons. As Ann Fienup-Riordan has noted with respect to the Yup'ik Inuit, "Nowhere did traditional Yup'ik ideology enshrine the Western distinction between dumb, mute animals in the service of human persons, with the latter only capable of possessing an immortal soul. On the contrary, the Yup'ik people considered animals to have originally been capable of transformation into creatures like men. Similarly, men might descend to visit the animal spirit world, where they would be made visible as human persons."[32] Humans were not the culmination of other species, merely one possible embodiment of a cycle of transformations.

In a cosmology where animals and humans have souls and humans do not have dominion over animals but must be furtively watchful not to cause offence, history has distinctive contours. The Enlightenment conception that history evolves into the activities of jural persons is bypassed altogether if the opposable thumbs of humans are not better than – just different from – the claws of bears and hooves of caribou. A history of the persons on Nuna would include the various ways that humans have violated or respected taboos and animals have responded.

Illustrating the dependence of history on cosmology, the traditional Inuit would give a different account of what happened to the beluga whale. The Inuit account would be based on a concept of animal agency that upsets the Qallunaat understanding of instrumentality. The Inuit perception is evident in an elder Inuk hunter's account of why the animals have become "wilder." Wild is the complement of tame for the Inuit. The newborn of any species are tame, and they remain so if the hunter is careful not to disturb them before they have had an opportunity to rest at their feeding places. Wild animals are alert to the presence of hunters and more cautious. They have become clever at concealing themselves and escaping. The elder noted that "animals are, for a wonder, getting wilder. The ones that can get wilder are the ones that could lay eggs and had their eggs taken. When animals get wilder, they seem to get less and less ... The word *nojuk* is a proper Eskimo word. When they are becoming *nojuk*, they are becoming more scared of what is done to them by guns. They are careful of the reckless hunters now, but the people before them were careful not to scare away the animals. Now this [noise] is a reason for animals seeming to become less."[33] Even a conventional natural history would leave out the critical explanatory dimension of how animals and humans relate within a shared psychological space. The toponym "Nunavik" does not capture that landscape.

The difference between Qallunaat and Inuit cosmologies also affects the literary conventions of historiography. Qallunaat clearly distinguish autobiography, myth, and history. The Inuit demarcation between legitimate and illegitimate history would not have been in the same place. Inuit cosmology goes some way to account for the findings of anthropologists puzzled by story-tellers who, when recounting tales of supernatural encounters which are the heritage of their people as a whole, told the stories as extensions of their own personal history.[34] Further, factual events in the Qallunaat historical record are sometimes described as supernatural encounters. Hence Inuit recorded, through stories of the supernatural, the history of the sometimes bloody encounters between the Thule and Dorset Inuit.[35]

Another implication flowing from Inuit cosmology is that not only human beings told history. A history requiring opposable thumbs for its recording would provide a meagre synopsis of the past. Animals, as persons, were just as likely to have an idea of history as humans, although reading this history would take a fair degree of attention – the kind alluded to by the elder in his remark that older generations of hunters were careful not to make the animals wild.

Not surprisingly, with the destabilization of these fixed points of Qallunaat historiography – space, the person, the historical record – the concept of time does not stand still. Time is one of the pivots of western historical consciousness. It, with topography, made up Collingwood's criteria for distinguishing historical writing from fiction. But the convention of minutes, days, and hours had no more "reality" on Nuna than a geographical schema based on metes and bounds. The chronology of Nuna was neither linear nor progressive. Bernard Saladin d'Anglure described Inuit chronology as grounded in circular space-time, adding that in the latter, "both the past and the future were ahead as well as behind, as were both captured and potential game animals, and, from an adult's point of view, both infants and ancestors. Nothing was stable or absolute in daily life; as in the myths everything was in process and transformation: distinctions between humans and animals, distinctions of scale, distinctions between dead and alive."[36] The cultural embodiment of time conditions the concept of history.

Referencing everything to a single chronology is one of the several assumptions that facilitates the idea that the absence in a people of a history standardized to Qallunaat conventions indicates the absence, in these people, of history. This blind spot promotes the idea that there is only one history of which the court need take judicial notice.

NUNA TO NUNAVIK

Another projection of time that makes it difficult to write cultural history is a convention from the study of culture: anthropology's exploitation of the ethnographic present. This literary device renders accounts of other people in the present tense – "the Inuit are a nomadic people" – thereby making deviations from the norms of one epoch departures from authenticity.

Fixing Inuit culture at the period of the ethnographer's fieldwork ignores the unceasing dynamism of groups that are constantly forming and reforming in the grip of the contingencies of time. Such ahistorical depictions prevent the Inuit from sharing the present with us. The "real" Inuit are the ones who lived on Nuna. Because their biological ancestors do not live by the same conventions as the Inutuinnait, the Inuit are no longer quite themselves.

On this version of cultural change, the judge might choose, some night when she returns to the Kuujjuaq Inn after a wearying week of court, to flip through a condensed history of the Inutuinnaitmiut of Nuna. It would be something she might do instead of going to the bar or flicking on the television. She might even congratulate herself on this burst of industriousness. She would not consider it part of her duties under s.20.0.8 of the 1976 James Bay Agreement, which states that "all judges and other persons appointed to dispense justice in the judicial district of Abitibi shall be cognizant with the usages, customs and psychology of the Inuit people." Nuna was shaped by circumstances that no longer prevail, its distinctive history hardly relevant for today's court.

It is tempting to fill in the time between Nuna and Nunavik with a progression of disappearances, the Inuit merging with a monocultural "we." This understanding has some resonance for those trying to keep the various forms of imperialism at bay. Part of the difficulty in outlining a continuity between Nuna and Nunavik is the asymmetry of power that has characterized Inuit/Qallunaat relations. This discrepancy is engraved in the very fact that it is non-Inuit institutions which make things like maps official. Inuit culture has been heavily impinged upon by larger social processes, an alien common sense insensibly internalized. In the face of this asymmetry, some reach for a parallel, internally coherent Inuit history, unshaped by this asymmetry, which needs to be salvaged and revivified.

The complacence that attending to difference is no longer necessary does not follow from a recognition of the wide spread of Qallunaat culture nor from the intransigence of its conventions. Such ethnocentrism (as well as the converse search for an Inuit culture that stands completely outside of world history) tends to under-emphasize the reciprocity in Inuit/Qallunaat relations, a reciprocity often structured by the imbalance of power. Wittgenstein's metaphor of the river and the riverbed is more apt: "I distinguish between the movement of the waters on the river-bed and the shift of the bed itself; though there is not a sharp division of the one from the other ... And the bank of that river consists partly of hard rock, subject to no alteration or only to an imperceptible one, partly of sand, which now in one place now in another gets washed away, or deposited."[37] Both cultures move dynamically forward. Nunavik alters the standards of official toponymy.

Cultures do not incorporate foreign elements holus-bolus. Foreign elements are naturalized in different ways. The object itself does not determine how it will be used in a new environment in the same way that an inuksuk could be an art object, a marker for hunters, or a simple pile of rocks, depending on the practices that revolve around it. Similarly, the internal restructuring of a culture does not happen by dint of force alone, because something that compels can be met with adaptation or despair, incorporation or resistance. The reaction contains the force and, like the vessel to water, contributes to its shape. This reciprocity is present, though it is much harder to recognize, in periods when one culture runs, like a spent trickle, down the immense, tempered, dam-like wall of another.[38]

The continuity between Nuna and Nunavik has these elements of reciprocity. The fur trade between the Inuit and Qallunaat is illustrative of this reciprocal, and asymmetrical, exchange. From the seventeenth to the early twentieth century the Inuit traded fur for things like rifles, cloth, tea, and flour. Neither the price of furs nor the configuration of power between the two groups remained constant over this period. Coming to agreement about the price of fur depended upon negotiations, and occasionally confrontations, about the relative worth of things in the respective systems for identifying assets. The price was not prefigured in either isolated economy. If the Inuit had valued white fox fur as the Qallunaat valued gold, the prices would have settled differently. In fact the Inuit did not prize the white fox, for meat or for fur, and rifles greatly facilitated their ability to hunt more desirable animals, less desirable to the Qallunaat.

At some point each economy had to accept the durable elements of the other's as a given. This lent stability to disputes about this particular fur or that specific rifle. This mutual incorporation of values made it increasingly difficult to speak of either economy in isolation. It belies Jenness's comment that the Qallunaat economy "destroyed [Eskimo] independence by replacing with manufactured goods the tools and weapons, the stone cooking-vessels and the skin boats that they could make from local materials with their own hands."[39] The notion of an *authentic* Inuit economy overlooks the fact that what makes something a local *good* is that it has a local *usage*. If an object does not have a local usage, it is not a *good* but rather an object as useless as fermented seal blubber to a society in which the product inspires distaste.

It would be a misrepresentation to claim, on the basis of the mutual settlement of practices, that each party had the power to manipulate without limit the worth of things within their own or the other's economy. While objects do not have worth outside of economies, the worth they have within them is as real as hunger. The Inuit cannot independently get the fur trade off the ground with fox fur at its current value. The stability of the core values of an economy is not set by individual negotiators but rather assumed and reinforced by them. What negotiators find themselves up against will determine the extent to which other values must yield. The givenness of this distribution of power can be seen in the relationship between the Inuit and fur traders.

The material aspects of a trapping/trading economy to a great extent exclude the demands of a fishing and hunting economy. Jenness spent a winter with two families of Inuit trappers at the turn of the century and recounted the competing demands of each practice:

In the first days of November, before they had laid out their lines of fox-traps … their nets ceased to yield the usual quota of fish and hung empty … From then on, my hosts devoted all their days to trapping. Every morning when the weather permitted they left the cabin before dawn, and returned at dark, or an hour later, after completing the round of their traps … Only twice down to the end of February … did we come upon the tracks of a polar bear near our cabin; never once did we see the hoof-prints of a caribou; and only twice, as far as I can remember, small flocks of ptarmigan … [O]ur excursions did not carry us more than about ten miles from our cabin.[40]

A good part of these material conditions were not made by the Inuit, nor by the Qallunaat. The environment contributed to the limits within which human manipulation was possible. Furthermore, by the time that Jenness lived with the Inuit, the use of rifles had considerably depleted the number of caribou and other traditional food sources, and whaling had decimated the Arctic whale population. These realities, combined with intermittent famines that ravaged the fishing and hunting economy every ten to fifteen years, made it reasonable for the Inuit to gravitate around trading posts. Further, the Hudson Bay Company, recognizing that hunting and fishing detracted from the energy required to maximize fur returns, buoyed the Inuit up with credit over the white fox's four-year cycle of scarcity and plenitude.

The credit economy set out a new limiting range of negotiating manoeuvers. Inuit ability to exploit credit was dependent on the worth of credit to the traders. This value was determined by the traders' relation to other elements of the economy.

Despite Britain's royal charter of 1670 conferring a monopoly on the Hudson's Bay Company, other traders worked the Eastern Arctic. The French company Révillon Frères was the company's main competitor. As a result of the competition, the company's ability to set the price of fur was constrained: the Inuit had a degree of mobility within the territory and could move to a more favourable post. Thus the credit expended to lure the Inuit into a steady trade had a pay-off.

When the Hudson's Bay Company finally absorbed Révillon Frères in 1936, it was able to make its posts the centre of economic gravity. The value of furs depreciated during the Great Depression in the South. With this combination of events, the Inuit thereafter retained very little ability to negotiate the worth of fox furs, which tumbled from a high price of $39 between 1924 and 1928 to $12 following the merger. Posts that until then had distributed credit in periods of scarcity closed at the convenience of the company, leaving the surrounding Inuit destitute.

The Inuit did not disappear with this wrenching change in circumstance any more than they traded themselves in when they traded hunting for trapping. Their presence on the land took on a different cast; their increasing powerlessness in the fur trade, aggravated by its collapse, permeated the subsequent tone of disputes between Qallunaat groups vying for control of the territory. The Inuit were less reckoned with than manipulated in the practices of more influential powers.

Nonchalance towards the Inuit on the ground can be seen in the dispute leading to the 1939 *Re Eskimos* case between the federal and Québec governments over administrative control of the territory.[41] With the demise of the fur trade and the depletion of traditional food stocks, the Inuit were in great need of relief in the form of food and supplies. This the federal government parsimoniously distributed through RCMP and trading posts. While the need for intervention rose, intergovernmental jurisdiction over the Inuit remained unsettled. During the Depression Québec and the federal government were anxious to unload the costs of relief onto each other, Québec arguing that the Eskimos were Indians – thus a federal responsibility under the constitution – and Ottawa stressing differences with Indians that made the Inuit citizens like any other. In 1932 the federal government asked the Québec government to refund its relief disbursements. Québec complied but served notice that it would not continue to do so.

The argument was referred to the Supreme Court of Canada in 1935 and decided in favour of the provincial government in 1939. It was held that the term "Indian" under head 24 of s.91 of the Constitution Act, 1867 included Eskimo inhabitants of the Province of Québec. Indians fell under federal jurisdiction. For the purposes of allocating relief costs, the Inuit were not a mere collection of individuals, indistinguishable from other individuals in the province: they were an Aboriginal *people*. As relief became institutionalized after the Second World War, the federal government thus inherited the delivery of social services in northern Quebec. If there were wider implications of construing the Inuit as a collectivity, they lay dormant.

The ease with which the Inuit were regarded as pawns is also evident in federal government policies aimed at including the Inuit within the body politic of the state while exploiting that inclusion to emphasize the state's frontiers to foreign governments. By the 1920s, sovereignty in international law was recognized as the exclusive right to display, over a portion of the globe, the functions of a state.[42] From this period on Canada's territorial sovereignty over the Arctic Archipelago was challenged by countries like Norway, Denmark, and the United States. Canada signalled its sovereignty by sending up patrolling ships and opening post offices and police detachments. The importance of semblance over substance is exemplified in the 1926 opening of a post office and RCMP detachment at Bache Peninsula on Ellesmere Island, previously uninhabited and contacted once a year by a ship which often could not get within miles of the post.[43]

Displaying the activities of state was also accomplished by strategically relocating the Inuit, who, as the beneficiaries of state policy, marked the outer limits of Canadian jurisdiction. In the 1950s, with little regard for the nuances of Inuit ecology and economy, Inuit from the Hudson coast of Nunavik were moved to the dark and inhospitable high Arctic. This "experiment" ambiguously aimed to deal with the destitution of the ruined trapping economy and to make a tangible contribution to Canadian sovereignty.[44] The paucity of consultation that went into the relocations indicated that, if the Inuit could not muster the menace of a foreign state, sovereignty would be exercised over them, not with them.

The tradition of determining the political landscape of Nunavik in the absence of the Inuit made it normal for the Québec government to assume that wresting administrative control of the territory from the federal government in the 1960s might resemble the exercise of drawing up imperial maps in the seventeenth century: it would be a bipartite affair. But by this time the political, legal, and economic history of the region had carved out and reinforced the distinctness of the collectivity that now referred to itself as the *inuit kupaimiut*, the Inuit people of Québec.[45] The historical classification of the Inuit as pawns in these struggles was a sorry feature of the collectivity's identity and became a focus of their subsequent political struggles.

In a visit to Kuujjuaq in 1961, René Levesque, then a member of the Liberal government, remarked with alarm upon the anglicization of the Inuit and the prevalence of federally run institutions.[46] Québec's acquisition of underlying title to the territory in the 1912 Boundary Extension

Act remained a legal abstraction until the provincial government took day-to-day control on the ground. In 1963 the Direction Générale du Nouveau-Québec (DGNQ) was created as the provincial administrative body in the North. The central policy of the DGNQ was clear: to settle the question of political authority in northern Québec by dislodging federal bureaucrats.[47] By 1964 an accord in principle was signed between Québec and the federal government in virtue of which the latter was to begin to withdraw from northern Québec in 1970. Inuit response to the agreements between foreign powers about Inuit territory was no longer off the record. In the 1970 Neville/Robitaille commission established by the two levels of government to assess the transfer of jurisdiction, the Inuit declared their resentment about being passed from one colonial government to another, the "little government" of Québec.[48] Inuit resistance accumulated more force as it headed into the events leading to the James Bay and Northern Quebec Agreement (JBNQA) of 1976.

The DGNQ was formed under the Ministry of Natural Resources – not an incidental grouping. In 1965, the first studies on the resource potential of the North were launched under this ministry, especially the potential for hydro power.[49] An economic base was essential if the Québécois were to become "*maîtres chez nous.*" By the 1970s hydro power was regarded not only as an inexpensive, reliable source of energy but as a symbol, capable of galvanizing human energy in southern Québec towards economic and social independence.

Inuit resistance to provincial plans to reduce the North to a provincial satellite through hydro development took the South by surprise. In the spring of 1971, the premier of Québec announced the construction of the hydroelectric project at James Bay and the creation of the Société de Développement de la Baie James, with a mandate to negotiate the expropriation of Native lands. The Inuit of the Hudson Coast formed Inuit Tungavingat Nunamini, a dissident movement to the cession of Inuit lands to the provincial government, and those on the Ungava coast formed the Northern Québec Inuit Association (NQIA). The latter joined with the Cree of northern Québec and became the officially recognized representative of Inuit interests in the dispute over northern resource extraction.

As the province proceeded with preliminary infrastructure development, the NQIA and northern Québec Cree sought an interlocutory injunction, *Kanatewat v. James Bay Development Corporation,* claiming that Indians and Inuit had an interest in the land that required a treaty to effect surrender.[50] Albert Malouf, the presiding judge, found in favour of the Aboriginal inhabitants and granted the injunction, noting that Aboriginal title to the territory had never been extinguished.

One week after this decision the Québec Court of Appeal overturned the injunction on a balance of convenience test, arguing that the development of hydroelectric power was of capital importance for ensuring the economic future and well-being of the citizens of Québec and that the interests of the entire "population québécoise" were represented by the James Bay Corporation.[51] As Natives were taken to have "évolué rapidement vers un mode de vie qui est celui de tous les Québécois," the interests of the "population québécoise" included those of the Natives.[52] The inconvenience to this larger population outweighed inconveniences caused to Natives who, in any event, the court maintained, held dubious legal title to the land.

Despite the appeal-court decision, the success at first instance put the NQIA and their Cree counterpart in a strong position to compel a negotiated agreement with the federal and provincial government. Despite the court of appeal's speculations, the law of Aboriginal title in Canada was far from settled in 1973. It was by no means certain that the Supreme Court of Canada would uphold the appeal court's understanding. With this leverage of uncertainty, the Inuit and Cree negotiated the James Bay and Northern Québec Agreement in 1976.[53]

With the JBNQA, the majority of Inuit accepted the extinguishment of Inuit title in the territory in exchange for monetary compensation, local governance, and limited control over the land. The JBNQA thus asserts in s. 2.1 that "In consideration of the rights and benefits herein set forth in favour of the James Bay Crees and the Inuit of Québec, the James Bay Crees and the Inuit of Québec hereby cede, release, surrender and convey all their Native claims, rights, titles and interests, whatever they may be, in and to land in the Territory and in Québec, and Québec and Canada accept such surrender." Through this cession, release, surrender and conveyance, Québec acquired the right to use the resources of the territory and to otherwise exploit it "for the benefit of all its people."[54]

The agreement split the territory into three categories of land, with different rights and obligations for Inuit and Qallunaat on each. The Inuit were left with one per cent of the land (Category I lands) over which they had extensive and exclusive rights and control. On a second parcel of land (Category II lands) they retained partial rights such as the exclusive ability to hunt, fish, and trap; these practices would have to be respected in the event of resource extraction. On the largest part of the territory (Category III lands) resource extraction would be able to proceed without Inuit permission while Native priority in harvesting remained.

The Inuit also retained immediate administrative authority on the local and regional level. So, for example, the agreement provides for an autonomous educational commission. It provides for municipal and regional control of economic development. Regional government has jurisdiction over, among other things, transportation, communications, health, social services, and the environment. The importance of cultural recognition in the domains of hunting, fishing, trapping, education, and justice was also underlined. These new powers allowed the Inuit to take over previously federal and provincial jurisdictions. The Inuit, little able to shape the past, strategically interpreted it in a way that could shape the future.

Although Inuit historical consciousness was destabilized by confrontations with Qallunaat historical consciousness, it was quite self-consciously restabilized following the agreement. This renewed identity was different from the unreflective transmission of culture that transpired while watching an *ulu* cut into a ringed seal or learning stillness at a seal breathing hole. It was alert to other menaces on the landscape. Informed by this new wariness, the Inuit undertook a number of cultural renewal projects in the years following. These included the resurrection of personal names which had been effaced from public life by unilingual Anglophones, the transcription of the minutiae of traditional practices into the written record, and the production of an Inuktitut dictionary. The place-name project was one of these undertakings. The limits of this inquiry would capture the homeland of the *inuit kupaimiut*: Nunavik.

The JBNQA promotes a particular version of the future of the territory based on the multiple conceptions of its past which converged in the negotiation process. As with any map, there is a gulf between its potential, abstract space and the practical space of journeys actually being made. The implementation of the agreement tends to slip into the tenacious stability of prior historical relations. The federal and provincial governments have been slow to implement some of the provisions of the agreement. Furthermore, it is not always clear what constitutes the "usages, customs and psychology of the Inuit people." This discrepancy between the abstract text and its object is nowhere more evident than in the sections on justice that promote the recognition of Inuit cultural identity.

STREAMS OF JUSTICE

The legal history of northern Québec recapitulates the struggle for dominion over Nunavik. The law was a powerful symbol of authority. As Morrison notes, the RCMP with their "long patrols ... dramatic confrontations with the Inuit ... planting of flags, and explanation of the King's law" were well suited to the public display of sovereignty.[55] But from the moment the first annual police patrol stepped into northern Québec in 1922 to the June circuit of 1992, there has been a gap between law's exhibition of authority and its local legitimacy.

The symbolic dimension of law in the North can be seen in the ranking of duties of the early RCMP in the North. Their paramount duty was, as outlined by the head of the Arctic division, "firstly, to uphold and enforce Canada's Sovereignty of her Arctic Islands."[56] They were sent to the North to guard the main entrances to Canada's Eastern Arctic and to cordon off the North symbolically from foreign claims to the territory. Posts were planted with an eye on foreign designs and with indifference to the presence (or absence) of Inuit inhabitants on the territory; thus the RCMP post at Bache Peninsula, set up at a place devoid of human beings who might generate conflict.[57]

Throughout the twentieth century Qallunaat planted police – or some other symbol of the law – like inuksuit. When the American military opened a base at Kuujjuaq during the Second World War in 1942, the federal government quickly opened an RCMP post in the community and reopened its Inukjuaq post.[58] In 1961 when the Québécois began supplanting federal institutions in the North with fleur-de-liste symbols, the provincial police force, the Sureté du Québec, was sent as the vanguard of the administrative state. The more conspicuous presence of the provincial court on the territory after 1970, with its flying circuits, was similarly capable of producing the desired effect.

From beginning to end of these displays of authority, there was an attempt to bring the Inuit within the moral ambit of the law. So, for example, in a 1919 Northwest Territories case, one of the lawyers argued that "These remote savages, really cannibals, the Eskimos of the Arctic have got to be taught to recognize the authority of the British Crown ... It is necessary that they should understand that they are *under the law* ... that they must regulate their lives and dealings with their fellow men, of whatever race ... according to ... the main outstanding principles of that law, which is part of the law of civilization."[59] Similarly, George

Binney informed the Inuit in *The Eskimo Book of Knowledge* that imperial law utterly filled the presumed legal vacuum:

You should know therefore that if one of your people is accused of committing a serious crime against the Laws ... *on no account* should that man be punished by your people in any way ... For ... if you punish that man you are also guilty of a crime and you are likely also to be punished for breaking the Law ... [T]he policeman will take the accused man and lead him before a wise man appointed by the King to uphold the Laws; and if it can be proved that the prisoner has broken the Laws ... then the wise man ... sternly orders the prisoner to be punished. But if it cannot be proved that the prisoner has broken the Laws ... then the wise man ... declares the prisoner to be "not guilty," and he commands the policeman to release him. This is justice. Throughout all parts of the world men of all countries admire British justice.[60]

Despite their grand seriousness, these pronouncements had dubious relevance. The small bearing of these postures on the Inuit can be partly explained by the tenuous presence of Qallunaat legal institutions in the territory. Until the circuit court began its tour of the North in 1970, southern law was so discontinuously distributed that it was disconnected from the daily life of the Inuit. The RCMP were infrequently available to the Inuit due to their limited patrols which did not follow Inuit land use patterns but rather the designs of foreign governments.[61] There were understandably few statistical reportings of Inuit crimes in the first half of the century, and in the limited number of cases where crimes were reported to the RCMP, they were dealt with locally by the police.[62] The full-blown spectacle of Qallunaat law was at best feebly simulated in Nunavik.

For the most part the Inuit dealt with disruptive behaviour themselves and in their own fashion. Inuit law may have been officially outlawed, but it was tolerated in practice as long as the extroverted vocation of the law, as an international symbol of sovereignty, remained unjeopardized. The continued pertinence of strictly Inuit law for the resolution of disputes has enabled legal anthropologists to describe, late into the twentieth century, features of Inuit legal practices quite incongruous to the Qallunaat legal order.

Several central distinctions between the two legal sensibilities derived from the different relationship between the individual and the group in each society. The Qallunaat concept of the autonomous jural person was illuminated by a theory of will and moral action which casts disruptive behaviour in a particular light. The notion of discrete, separate loci of self-control was not as congenial to the Inuit. This is evident in forms of speech and self-reference. As Jean Malaurie noted, "seul le groupe permet à l'homme de vivre. L'homme ainsi protégé, réserve, en retour, à la société, sa force et sa pensée. Au point que, refoulant toute réaction individuelle, il ne s'explique qu'à la troisième personne, se coulant dans une pensée générale, celle du groupe. Jamais un Esquimau ne dit: je pense, mais les 'Inouit' pensent."[63] The concept of the person derived in part from the relationship of the group to the world. The landscape and its demands significantly structured group identity and militated against individualism. From this flowed significant legal consequences.

During her experience in the field in the 1960s, Jean Briggs was struck by the strong social pressures against the expression of individual needs and emotions: "emotional control is highly valued among Eskimos; indeed, the maintenance of equanimity under trying circumstance is *the* essential sign of maturity, of adulthood."[64] The expression of anger and other self-oriented emotions was costly and had to be suppressed. Consequently, passive and silent withdrawal by the group from the individual was a subtle manner of correcting deviance without a disruptive drama of emotion. It was also devastatingly effective in light of the material and psychological unsuitability of the individual to survival on the land.

Briggs's own experience is illustrative. When she went in 1963 to live with a small group of Inuit at the mouth of the Back River, she experienced the corrective power of ostracism. Dropped by plane and left alone to do her anthropological research, she was adopted by an Inuk family who were part of a group of twenty to thirty-five Inuit, the sole inhabitants of an area of 35,000 square miles. After months of living with this family, she lost her temper (very mildly by southern standards) at some passing Qallunaat who had broken one of the Inuit canoes. As a result of her volatility, she was "ostracized, very subtly, for about three months. During this period there was simply no use in asking questions. At best, Utku consider questions boorish and silly; nevertheless, they will sometimes politely attempt to answer them. During this period of tension, however, they did not."[65] Three months of this takes a toll on an outsider whose fate is mitigated by the next flight out, more so for one whose dependence on the group is complete.

The threat of the group picking up camp in a matter of hours and disappearing while one was out hunting allowed a great degree of psychological subtlety in sanctions. As Norbert Rouland noted, "au niveau de la sanction du droit, ce principe sociologique a pour effet que l'opinion publique joue un rôle prépondérant dans l'application des procédures destinées à recitifier un comportement déviant. Exprimant le jugement du groupe – que certains maïeutes peuvent aider à se dégager – elle est souveraine."[66] The public construction of events became darkly ominous in the shadow of abandonment.

Inuit sanctions were both psychological and diffuse. They were not localized in one set of persons; a permanent hierarchy of power was unfamiliar to Inuit societies.[67] Deducing the absence of public authority from the absence of formal leaders and officials would be a mistake. As Rouland noted, "le groupe, directement ou par l'intermédiaire de certaines autorités, intervient très activement dans les processus de contrainte juridique, soit en posant des limitations aux modes privés de solution des conflits au nom de l'intérêt public, soit en mettant en œuvre de véritables types d'action publique."[68] The mechanisms of enforcement were non-nucleated and no particular individual or group was clearly responsible for maintaining order.

The diffuse nature of Inuit sanctions across the group did not preclude more formal dealings with disruptive behaviour and explicit sanctions. Hoebel and Balikci observed in the 1940s and '60s gatherings of the whole group to consider more drastic interventions than ostracism, derision, and gossip where the behaviour of an individual posed a grave threat to the entire camp.[69] Sometimes decisions to banish or execute the offender resulted.

The importance of the group also explained behaviours of the Inuit that would have been criminal in the South. The acceptability of some forms of murder among the Inuit derived from the need for group survival.[70] Infanticide, invalidicide, senilicide, and suicide by the aged were acceptable, indeed sometimes expected.[71] The notion of individual rights opposable to the group had little currency.

The primacy of the group for the Inuit had bearing on other legal domains than sanction. The small size of the group in conjunction with the importance of its construction of disruptive behaviour would render nonsensical the Qallunaat exclusion of hearsay evidence – statements by a witness of what he had heard someone else say. Not only was the act and the offender of necessity well known in a group of several dozen human beings living in intimate quarters but gossip about the event was exploited as a sanction. To take away hearsay would be to take away the power of the group.

The Qallunaat convention of excluding similar-fact evidence – evidence of the accused's discreditable conduct on past occasion – would also be peculiar in this setting. Intimate knowledge of the character and previous actions of each member of the group was unavoidable; the personal history of an offender dwelt in the collective memory of the group. Such an exclusion would have amounted to an eradication of collective memory and would also have undermined the social manipulation of such knowledge in the re-establishment of the social order.

The importance of the group also indicated the lesser relevance of the absence of harmful intent or *mens rea*. If the stability of the community had been disturbed, therein lay the offence. An internal state of mind paled next to the public impact of the event. Determining the nature of the crime was less a matter of locating intent than assessing the impact of the act. The actual offence was a starting point for the re-establishment of communal order, not the occasion for retrospective and introspective speculation.

The place of the group in nomadic Inuit life meant that explicit, codified sanctions administered hierarchically were neither familiar nor necessary. Behaviour was normalized in a manner suitable to the physical and social environment. This setting, as we have seen, was not immutably fixed.

Most significantly, after the 1950s the Inuit became predominantly sedentary around the trading and police posts, moving into permanent homes, complementing traditional activities with state benefits. State control came wed to these benefits. So, for example, when schools were established at the posts in the 1950s, the Inuit were informed that they had to cease bringing their children onto the land to hunt and trap for the duration of the school year. Failure to comply meant that their family allowance cheques could be withheld.[72] The complexion of social interactions changed as the day-to-day landscape – physical and social – changed. Further, the web of interactions came to include those in whom Inuit dispositions had never been inculcated.

The Inuit were not only coerced into changing their modes of social control; they actively appropriated elements of legal administration that met Inuit needs and grafted them onto Inuit legal practices. So, for example, banishment – the Inuit sanction for recalcitrant offenders – was enhanced by RCMP intervention and incarceration. Nelson Graburn, an American legal anthropologist, may have overstated the case in 1969 by relating that "[b]y far the most common reaction in post-World

War II Eskimo society is 'leave it to the white man.'"[73] This is belied by
the persistent difficulty that Qallunaat administrators faced in getting
the Inuit to use the law within southern terms of reference, yet his
remark is nonetheless indicative of the Inuit naturalization of Qallunaat
practices. Inuit law began to harmonize with Qallunaat law, but this was
not a one-way change. Both legal systems had elements that, now in one
place, now in another, got washed away or deposited, and elements that
were subject to no alteration or only to imperceptible ones.

If the Inuit incorporated new norms, Qallunaat legal officials, no
doubt due to their mandate in the North, were less ingenious with local
custom. Qallunaat administrators were persistently self-conscious about
their blundering inability to make southern law mean what they wanted
it to in the North. The comments of a northern administrator to the
deputy minister of Justice in 1945 are illustrative. He suggested that "[i]f
each Eskimo were given a chevron to attach to his parka if his record
was good, with perhaps a different coloured chevron for any outstanding
achievement, the removal of these chevrons would constitute a punishment which would probably be appreciated. The holder of ten chevron
might receive an annual grant of some nature that would be sought
after."[74] Of course, what was instrinsically sought after by the Inuit was
precisely what had eluded the Qallunaat in compelling obedience in the
first place.

Corporal punishment was also suggested as a special measure to deal
with the Inuit. The same northern administrator commented that the
only way to punish an Inuk was to humiliate him, making him lose face
in the eyes of his community. In cases of homicide, he suggested that the
guilty Inuk be publicly whipped in front of the whole community. He
added that one who had endured such a shame would not immediately
react in defence, but to eradicate such dishonour he would seek to kill
the author of the punishment. Consequently, the punishment should
not be inflicted by the local police but administered by a special envoy
from the South. Local police "would probably be ambushed and killed
even though it took years to accomplish."[75]

Qallunaat were further hampered in their ability to incorporate local
practices by their persistent perception of the Inuit as lacking in historical consciousness and thus irrationally motivated. The Inuit were perceived as embryonic Qallunaat. In 1921 the RCMP commented on "des
conditions tout à fait primitives dans lesquelles vivent ces indigènes et
... leur ignorance des lois."[76] This perception of the Inuit as lacking in
legal sensibility was reiterated by the judge of an infamous Belcher Island

case of 1941.[77] Four accused were charged with murder, having killed nine members of a small community in a religious frenzy while convinced that they were God and Jesus. The court, on this rare occasion, flew up with all of its attendant spectacle. A marquee was brought up from Ottawa and covered with a large Union Jack, a picture of the royal family hung beside the judge's chair, a small Union Jack hoisted on a pole near the entrance to the marquee.[78] In sentencing the accused, the judge remarked:

These Eskimos are, in fact, still in an early stage of evolution as human beings … [Applying] the Criminal laws of Canada – the white man's law – to the primitive Eskimos of these Islands … is a delicate task, because these people, though in some aspects of their behaviour very childlike … are in many other aspects of their behaviour very childish – of low mental growth judged by our standards … The task is also a difficult task because we are here seeking to apply to a primitive people, who to a large extent have lived without the law, the moral standard and concepts of organized civilized society.[79]

The Inuit, apparently, had nothing like a legal system that might enhance Qallunaat interventions.

Concocting an innovative system of rewards and punishments was conceived of as one way of forcing the Inuit into the body politic of Canada. Abandoning the notion of pan-Canadian criminal law was another. In the fallout from the Belcher Island case, which attained a degree of notoriety in the South, the latter policy was contemplated by several northern justice administrators who recommended that the Criminal Code be applied to the Inuit with discretion, depending on their proximity to "civilization." The adjustment of the criminal law to the "backwardness" of the Inuit was a common and persistent policy.

Embarking on a pedagogical campaign to educate the Inuit about southern legal standards was another favoured policy. An RCMP agent outlined this program in 1947 when he remarked that the state had to "increase police supervision to educate the Inuit about Southern legal habits."[80] The increased police presence on the territory in the following years was part of a program aimed at filling in the Inuit legal void.

The inability to perceive the Inuit as having legal and historical consciousness was exacerbated by the agenda of sovereignty in the North. To a considerable extent the law's primary mission on the territory was as a beacon of political authority, its signal directed to external governments. This preoccupation with powers beyond Nunavik was carried into provincial involvement in northern Québec. The sq were sent to northern Québec in 1961 as the vanguard of the new administration. Shortly thereafter, criminal regulation of the Inuit rose precipitously. In 1968 the SQ initiated three criminal proceedings. In 1969, they initiated 140 complaints and carried through with twenty-three proceedings.[81] In 1970, the number of complaints rose to 179 with fifty-four proceedings. Until this time, the bulk of cases were tried in Montréal or Sept-Iles, though occasionally judges flew north to Poste-de-la-Baleine or Kuujjuaq.

In 1970 Justice Malouf of the Superior Court dismissed the *Ittoshat* case, which involved an Inuk from Poste-de-la-Baleine who had been charged with public disorder and flown from his community to Montréal for his trial. The judge noted that the accused was deprived of, among other things, the ability to make full defence, given that potential defence witnesses were hundreds of miles away. This decision provided some incentive for the creation of a court that could conduct local hearings. Other explanations have been advanced for the creation of the itinerant court of northern Québec in 1974.

The crisis of conscience of the *Ittoshat* decision served as one inspiration for the 1971 Choquette Commission, charged with studying the administration of justice in northern Québec.[82] This inspiration is evident in the commission's report, which confronts issues of racism and promotes the protection of an Aboriginal cultural sphere. The report addresses the recurring problems of the delivery of justice in the North – such as the trial and incarceration of Inuit offenders in faraway, culturally and linguistically alien settings. The institution of the commission, however, also postdated Premier Bourassa's 1971 announcement of the James Bay development project by a year and the Cree and Inuit application for an interlocutory injunction of the same by scarcely a month.

The struggle for political authority over Nunavik was not absent from the report of the commission, which included bureaucrats from the Ministry of Natural Resources as well as lawyers, police, and justice officials. Their report spoke to the enclosure of the Inuit within the frontiers – legal, moral, and cultural – of Québec. The authority of the law would serve as a vehicle for integrating the Inuit into the larger provincial population. Staffing Qallunaat legal institutions with Inuit personnel would facilitate this process: "If police duties are carried out by those belonging to the community, the people will more readily accept authority and obey the law. This principle is also an important factor in social integration."[83] The implicit reinforcement of the borders of Québec through legal interaction with the Inuit is evident in the provisions on policing: "Close contact with the native peoples can only increase the prestige of the police officer and the good name of Québec whose authority he represents. As a result, his task will be facilitated and he will be able to play a role as an educator, which must to some extent be added to his usual duties. By doing so, he will be able to increase the people's awareness of their responsibilities and their duties as citizens."[84]

The displacement of the court to the North beginning in the early 1970s augmented the prestige of southern law as well as Québec's reputation for political authority. The itinerant court inaugurated its northern voyages in the winter of 1974, just prior to the JBNQA.

The dual vocation of the law spelled out in the Choquette Commission – the affirmation of Inuit cultural and legal needs within the political aspirations of Québec – was also evident in the two chapters of the JBNQA devoted to the administration of justice in Nunavik. The delivery of justice remained under the auspices of the state via the accumulated jurisdictions of the Provincial Court, magistrates under the Criminal Code, Court of the Sessions of the Peace, Social Welfare Court, and one or two justices of the peace. The integration of the Inuit into this framework was outlined in the sections devoted to the training of Inuit personnel for these institutions. The agreement also noted that the administration of northern justice must be responsive to the "usages, customs and psychology of the Inuit people." Dense Qallunaat institutionalization, however, combined with the vagueness of these provisions, meant that cultural recognition could be fairly nominal while respecting the strict letter of the law.

Since the JBNQA, Inuit response to the southern legal system on their territory has been a complex mix of appropriation, resistance, toleration, and reciprocity. The use of the law as a symbol of political authority was not lost on the Inuit. In 1977 the Ungava Inuit undertook a large-scale protest against the provincial language policies of Bill 101 which promoted the use of the French language across Québec. They not only lowered fleur-de-lis, shut provincial schools, and cut off water delivery to the homes and offices of provincial employees in an effort to get them to leave but they also invited the provincial police to depart.[85]

A more spectacular revolt against southern law began in 1984 in Povungnituk (Pov). In that year the Pov Inuit called representatives from the itinerant court to a series of meetings to discuss the administration of justice. The Inuit drew attention to the inability of the court to contain conflicts in the North and to its various cultural blind spots.[86] Out of these meetings and under the guidance of Judge Jean-Charles Coutu – the judge who had inaugurated the itinerant court's first flight to the North – a proposal for a local justice committee was submitted to the Ministry of Justice in 1985. This group was to cooperate with the police and Crown prosecutor (and vice versa) in determining which cases ought to be handled by the southern legal system and which cases should be de-judicialized and handled locally. The Crown prosecutor was to retain ultimate discretion in the channelling of cases.

One month after this submission the community council of Pov approved an alternative project, the Novalinga/Tookalak project (named after its two main participants), and submitted it to the Ministry of Justice. At the heart of this proposal was local control of an *Inuit* justice system. The submission complained of the subjugation of Inuit culture inherent in the necessity of making appeals to a foreign legal system to resolve local conflicts. It remarked on the inadequacies of the itinerant court stemming from both its ephemeral presence and ignorance of Inuit culture. It recognized legal differences such as the Qallunaat weighting of individual punishment over community harmony. Where the Coutu project emphasized the de-judicialization of a specified list of cases, the Novalinga/Tookalak project emphasized extensive Inuit appropriation of the legal process.

The tension between these two visions came to a head just months after the respective proposals were submitted. In the summer of 1985 a juvenile Inuk broke into the post office and, during arrest, assaulted a police officer and threatened him with a firearm. He was deported to Amos in southern Québec, then released back to the community pending trial. The community, feeling that he was dangerous and disruptive, did not welcome his return and requested his continued detention in the South. The request was denied. Upon his return, the community incarcerated the youth in the local detention centre. This was not the first incarceration of its kind; the community had been feeling the effects of a wave of juvenile glue-sniffing and vandalism and had responded by imprisoning offenders.

The community was promptly informed by a judge of the itinerant court – à la Binney – that the incarcerations were illegal and that the incarcerators could be subject to charges of kidnapping and sequestration and liable to a five-year prison term. The allegations were aggravated by the fact that juvenile offenders require a special judicial process in the southern legal system and that glue-sniffing, destructive as it might be for an isolated northern community, was not a criminal offense.

This dispute was resolved by a joint undertaking by Judge Coutu, the Ministry of Justice, and community leaders to meet immediately following the juvenile's release to discuss the larger issues of control over the administration of justice. But the meetings failed to resolve whether the status quo, the Coutu proposal, or the Pov proposal would prevail. Facing the breakdown of negotiations, the minister of Justice hired two anthropologists from a private research centre to undertake an ethnographic study of the situation. A report from this inquiry, *La Justice en question,* was published one year later, in 1986.[87]

The Pov confrontation ultimately generated more study and recommendations than change. In addition to the anthropologists' study, Pov formed its own justice committee, the Sapuulutait, which submitted proposals to the Ministry of Justice. Judge Coutu also submitted a long and well-documented list of complaints and suggestions about the delivery of justice amongst the Inuit.[88] But Inuit discontent with Qallunaat justice has not substantially subsided since this time. It came again into focus with the Inuit Justice Task Force which consulted with Inuit communities in Nunavik between 1991–93.

The task force was given a mandate by Makivik to review the administration of justice in Nunavik. Although it heard diverse and at times contradictory responses from the communities, the following comments punctuated the critique like a refrain:

The present court system and police are utterly futile. The foreign system is run by Qallunaat and Inuit do not feel they own or control the system.

The values of the Inuit are degraded by having to follow the rules of Qallunaat.

Wipe out the present SQ Police – replace them with all Inuit, if possible.

We will never control our own justice affairs until we attain control and jurisdiction in justice.[89]

The task force concluded by recommending that the institutionalization of Inuit customary law within the present Qallunaat administration of justice was merely interim "until Inuit of Nunavik have their own justice system."[90]

While the task force heard comments about traditional Inuit justice and Inuit control over the legal system, the report is also scattered with comments such as:

Court should be able to deal with cases much more quickly. (Perhaps two courts are needed: Hudson and Ungava coasts.)

Small communities should be provided with the same quality of police as larger communities.

Inuit should abide by the laws of Canada. A lack of understanding of the laws of Canada cannot be used as an excuse for not respecting the law. But, on the other hand, a clear understanding of these laws does not presently exist.[91]

The desire for an increased Qallunaat legal presence appears to contradict the promotion of a distinctively Inuit legal system. This contradiction is, for the most part, only apparent. The Inuit have, throughout the presence of Qallunaat law on the territory, incorporated Qallunaat sensibilities into their local practices in the same manner that they incorporated manufactured goods into their economy. To the extent that the Inuit have actively used the police and the court, these institutions have become part of Inuit usages, customs, and psychology. This is not to claim that to the extent that the Inuit grafted Qallunaat legal practices onto their own they abandoned their own culture, any more than the court's responsiveness to local legal sensibilities is indicative of its degeneration.

Qallunaat responsiveness to the Inuit context can be traced through the history of the circuit court. A degree of reciprocity between Qallunaat and Inuit legal sensibilities has been perhaps most evident in Judge Coutu's struggles to make the legal system work within the Inuit context. His discomfort with the Qallunaat legal system in the North began in 1974 with the first flight of the itinerant court, when he admitted to feeling a little like an intruder. He speculated whether "il n'était pas préférable de laisser à ces peuples le soin de régler entre eux les problèmes de nature criminelle."[92] His struggle to bring equity to the delivery of justice in the North continued with the Coutu project coming out of the 1984 Pov demands and his critique of the administration of justice to the minister of justice following the 1986 crisis in Pov. It is also evident in his inviting community feedback in sentencing following a 1992 case on the Hudson coast – an unorthodox proposal in the southern legal system.

In the same year as this innovative court session, the June circuit of 1992 took place on the coast of Ungava. Both dockets reflect the embodiment, in the dispositions of those who attended, of the history I have outlined – the traces of dominion and subjugation, the tension between incorporating another culture and resisting it, the intermingling of sensibilities.

Throughout the history, it is not always clear what constitutes beneficial and what constitutes harmful accommodation. That the course of the history emerged within the constraints and injunctions of power makes such an assessment difficult both to make and to avoid. If there were no asymmetry in the relationship between the groups, no humiliation, no contemporary anguish, it might be easier to bless the history as a whole, as one might from one's deathbed. If all of the coercion led to resistance and all of the accommodation stemmed from circumspection, it might be easier to sort out which traditions should be carried forward for the next generation and which abandoned.

While the account of the June circuit that opened this book left a palpable sense of the awkward fit between the court's procedures and local practices – a sense for which I have here attempted to lay out the historical grounds – there was another troubling undercurrent to the evening which so far has remained below the surface. This is the relationship of force between men and women.

Violence against women is not an incidental element in projections about an equitable redistribution of legal resources in Nunavik. It would be premature to suggest a revision to the legal system on the basis of an Inuit/Qallunaat opposition without reckoning with the concrete details of which the injustice of family violence is composed. These details of people's lives are not often revealed in the procedural confines of the courtroom – though they may be felt in the wearying sense of return which the judge expressed in the opening narrative at seeing the same violent men return to him over and over again.

The next section presents two accounts of the experience of family violence, the first by a woman, the second by a man. Both were recounted to my co-worker, Louisa Whiteley, and myself as part of our investigation into family violence in Nunavik communities in the summer of 1992. The accounts were recorded and transcribed. The narrators then generously and courageously agreed to share the stories as part of a compilation of such accounts in a document on family violence in the North which was distributed throughout the community and to social and legal services. Certain details have been changed to preserve the anonymity of the story-tellers and the people about whom they speak.

The Children under the Bed

ONE

I have gone through an awful lot.* First of all I don't have parents. My father died when I was nineteen. And my mother died when I was ten. She left Kuujjuaq because she had tuberculosis. She never came back. They took her away to Montréal. She couldn't come back up North, so my father and I had to move to be with her.

That's when I first realized that there was a distinct difference between girls and boys. When my mother was in Montréal, my father also had to go away because he got TB. I was left all alone in Montréal, with no relatives, so they placed me in a boarding house which took in little girls. There was only one room with four girls and the beds were already occupied. Some of the girls were sleeping two to a bed. Since I was the oldest one I had to sleep in the same room as the house parent's two sons. The older brother used to come in after drinking and I would find him on top of me, trying to take off my clothes. I was about six years old. I was old enough to realize that something was wrong. I went to my house mother and she told me what to do the next time it he did it.

The next time, I decided that that was enough: I didn't like it. I told him I had to go to the bathroom and I sneaked into the little girls' room. I remember being grabbed by one arm by his mother and him grabbing me on the other arm and they were both trying to get me.

---

* This account and the one that follows are from *Family Violence in Kuujjuaq: Talking to Each Other,* ed. Susan G. Drummond and Louisa Whiteley (Kuujjuaq: Kuujjuaq Social Services, 1992).

That was the first time that I found out that a girl could get sexually abused by a guy. Fortunately for me they took me out of that house right away because the house mother had informed the authorities. After that, I returned to Quaqtaq to live with my aunt and her husband. We used to live in a very small house, no rooms, no nothing. Even the toilet was not private. We used to sleep on the floor. And right away, my aunt's husband suggested that he sleep between me and my aunt. I guess I should have realized then what was going to happen. I should have known because I had already experienced it. Ever since then he abused me sexually for a great many years – for maybe twenty years – ever since I was a little girl.

My aunt found out about that. I was ten years old. I hadn't told anybody up until then because he threatened to beat me up and to kill me if I told anyone. I would have liked to tell somebody but I liked my life too much. Even though I never said anything, my aunt found out on her own. She came in one night and my pants were down. My aunt didn't do anything about the abuse, though. My father also knew. They both didn't do anything. I felt abandoned. Sometimes I used to feel really alone.

My oldest two children are from my aunt's husband. Not because I wanted to but because I had to. I didn't have teenage years. I didn't have a young life. He got me pregnant when I was eighteen. I was nineteen when I had the first child. Somehow I managed to keep myself a virgin until I was seventeen. Somehow I managed. I always, always refused to let him penetrate me. He tried so hard to penetrate me. Sometimes I couldn't sit down and pee, he hurt me so badly.

At about that time I went down to Montréal. After I failed some of my classes, they sent me back home to Quaqtaq. I tried telling the Department of Northern Affairs about what was happening in my aunt's home. I didn't want to go back home. They sent me back anyhow. Maybe it was because of the times. They didn't know very much or do very much about sexual abuse in those days.

After I came back to Quaqtaq, the sexual abuse went on for a long, long time. Two of the children that I had by my uncle were adopted out and another child died. The last one died because my pregnancy was physically very hard for me. I was working all through my pregnancy. I was carrying pails of water and I was washing clothes by hand, washing my aunt's clothes. I was carrying the baby on my back, making bannock, doing the dishes … everything. The child was born prematurely. All the women in the village and the doctors told me that it was because I was working too hard. Only my aunt said it was because of something else. It went on for so long that I got sick and tired of it. I ran away to another community.

My aunt's husband also used to beat me up a lot too. Both him and her, they used to beat me up a lot. I think my aunt used to blame me for what he was doing to me, and the way she would take it out on me was by beating me up. And him, he was jealous. He was jealous of me seeing other boys since he first started trying to abuse me. I was like his possession since he started abusing me. My father wasn't really there for me either. I would say 10 to 15 per cent of the time he was there for me.

Everybody in the village knew that I was being abused. Everybody knew. Even people from other communities knew it was going on. My goodness, that used to make me feel so tiny, so very small. Everybody knew and nobody did anything about it. Maybe they thought that I loved it.

I still see that man. He is still alive and I still see him. I hardly say hi to him. I have a lot of anger towards him. I used to see him two times a week. Every time I see him, I don't want to say hi. I want to stick a knife in him. Maybe if I had talked about it when I was a child, it wouldn't make me feel so bad.

I have been told that I can press charges against the man now. But he is beginning to be an old man. His children are all grown up. He has always been in the open, in open spaces. His youngest son is ten to twelve years old. He asks his father out to do all sorts of things. I don't live with him any more. If I lived with him again, I would not be able to sleep through the night.

He is still abusing young girls. His twenty-one-year-old son seems to have the same problem. He started to do the same thing that his father was doing. Their oldest daughter is seven years old and I don't think he has touched her. But he is abusing another daughter. I told my friend to tell my aunt what her son is doing. My aunt didn't want us to tell anybody. Not the cops, not social services, not anybody else. She is protecting him. I wouldn't mind going back to that community and taking that little girl out.

Not too long after I ran away I started living with a guy. He was okay in the first few weeks. But one night he came in and started beating me up and I ended up in the hospital. The minister told me not to talk to the man, to leave him. But then the man came in and he was all sweet and I went back to him.

He beat me up again. He beat me up so many times. The first few times I had a black eye, I was too ashamed to go outside. I didn't want people to see me. It got so bad that I started realizing it was not my fault. I started going out. People starting noticing my black eyes. People started to tell me to leave him. He used to come inside the house and if I was sleeping, he would wake me up with a punch on the face. Or I used to come in from outside and he would greet me with a punch. Or he would come in and greet me with a punch. Sometimes he used to aim guns – with bullets in them – at me. Or use table legs. Or use his teeth. He used to give me diseases and put the blame on me.

In the beginning he was gentle and tender. And in between black eyes he was gentle and tender. Most of the time he was just degrading me. Even the cops used to come to the house and tell me to charge him, but I refused because I thought about what would happen if he came out of prison and was angry at me for putting him in jail. The cops used to come in and I would say everything was okay. The neighbors used to call the cops. They realized something was going on. They'd hear banging in the house and they'd realize that it was not just pots that were being thrown around. My son didn't like to see my boyfriend beat me up. Twice he had even beaten my son up with me. He was about seven years old at the time.

This man once beat me up with a caribou leg. The first few times that he used to beat me up, I used to yell and scream and tell him to stop. It always seemed as though it made it worse. It got to be so many times that he beat me up that I got used to it and I never uttered a sound. I didn't cry that time that he beat me up with a caribou leg. I started walking and I started crying.

The next day he told me to go and get hamburgers. We had drank the night before. I had had $300 in my pocket. I lost the money. Somebody took the money from my pocket. When he told me to go and get hamburgers, I knew that I wouldn't be able to buy any because I didn't have any money. If I told him I lost it he would have almost killed me. That was right after he beat me up with a caribou leg. I went out and I got some hamburgers. The store gave me the hamburgers because they could see I had been beaten up and that he was going to beat me again. When I brought the hamburgers in to him, he got up and he started to come towards me. He was clenching and unclenching his fists and I knew that he was going to beat me up again. So I ran out the door. I took one last look at the house and I said I am not going back inside. And I never did. I never went back inside that house.

I used to run away from him and go to other homes. He would always find me and take me back to the house. So as soon as I went out of the house, I started to think of where I could go so he wouldn't find me. I went to a doctor's house. He asked me if I wanted to leave for another community. I said yes, so he arranged for me to leave. That's how I got out of that situation.

The man followed me there. But I made it clear that I didn't want him there and he left. He knew that was it. I had left him for good. Even now, he has seen me a few times and he has let me know that he would be willing to have me back but I am not going.

I never had any feelings for him. The only feeling I ever seem to have is the one towards my kids. I love my kids and that is about it.

After I left that man, I met a Qallunak and I lived with him for a lot of years. I got four kids from him. It wasn't so bad in the sense that he didn't hit me physically. One time he did hit me and I hit him back. I let him know that I was not going to stand around while he was beating me up. Verbally and mentally, though, he was always pretty mean to me. He used to say I wasn't good enough for him, that I wasn't doing things right around the house.

Maybe sometimes men that I get involved with think they are using me but I am also using them. I don't use them for intimacy, never for intimacy or for respect. I tried to be intimate with this man and it backfired more than once. Whenever we had an argument he would bring up what I had told him. One time when I was pregnant with my daughter, he said a horrible thing to me. I had told him that one of my aunts was adopted. She was adopted because her mother died in childbirth. I told my husband that. I think that when women are pregnant, some of their mind helps form the mind of the child. So once, when I was pregnant we started arguing. All of a sudden he turned around and said that he hoped that when I was in labour, the same thing would happen to me as happened to the mother of my aunt. I felt terrible. He said it just like that. My daughter was born three weeks late because I thought when I went into labour, I would die in childbirth. It was very scary.

This man started accusing me of having my oldest son as my lover. That really hurt. He even wrote a letter to my son and said that because I had been a sexual abuse victim, I was going to abuse my children. He said that is the way that it usually works out: people who are abused will abuse children. He wrote me an even worse letter asking me why I bother going to church. He wrote that I should know that I am going to rot in hell forever because of what I was doing with my son. In the letter he wrote to my son, he said that our youngest child is my oldest son's daughter so that in fact my daughter is also my grandchild.

One time he accused me of having fifty-seven lovers. Another time that went up to 120. He would accuse me of this when he was drunk or sober. He told me that I had given him AIDS. But he was sleeping around on me. He slept with my best friend. That was a good excuse to get rid of him. For over two years he was accusing me of having my son as my lover. So I found a perfect situation to kick him out of the house.

One day, we went over to my friend's house for a roast. I came in late. Just before I finished eating, she asked him if he wanted to play a game of Scrabble. They could see that I was almost finished. I asked them to wait for me. They didn't want to wait for me. So I thought maybe they wanted to play by themselves. Little did I realize that I was right. I left early because my children wanted to go home. My friend was alone in the house. The rest of her family was out of town. He never came back home that night. I knew what he had done. He did the same thing the next night. He sneaked out of the house. I knew where he went. I knew that if I went in I would find him there. But I didn't want to go and see. Why should I have to see that? I didn't have any feelings for him. I left that situation right after I found out that he slept with my best friend. Now I'm here. It's been over a year since I left.

I would rather find a nice person. Somebody that I could talk to and be friends with, and also be lovers with. But it's never been that way because of the way I grew up. I never seem to have any feelings for the men that I get involved with. It's never from my heart. The men want sex. It was always that way when I was growing up. They just want sex. In my past it has always been wham bam. I think if I told men that I wanted to take my time … I don't know what would happen. I think only one man in one hundred would listen to that.

Sometimes I think my children miss a male in their lives. I would also want the person to be nice and caring and not beat up my children. If I did ever live with somebody that had sexually abused my children, I don't know what I would do. Even little boys are not left alone. I don't think there is any pleasure at that age either. I don't ever want it to happen to my children.

One other time I was very badly beaten by a man. He beat me unconscious. When I came around, the first question the doctor asked me was: "Why are you alive?" They had given me the last rites. I keep thinking that there must be something I have to do, or should do. My children keep me going. I know what it is like growing up without a mother. I don't want that to happen to my children. Sometimes I ask why I wasn't killed that night. I think that there must be a reason for me to live. I think that my children are what I live for now. Everything has always been for my children because they seem to be the only people that I have any feelings for.

TWO

Violence is a problem in a lot of the homes here. I see so many men in this town beating women. I say: look at that asshole, he beat up his wife again. And I'm doing it myself ... And I don't want to do it.

As far back as I can remember my father was a very violent person. He was always beating my mother or beating us kids. He was beating up on someone all the time.

My mom used to probably provoke a bit of it too. But she also put up with an awful lot as well. She stayed home. She had ten kids. She stayed home and sewed and made money any way she could to help. I don't remember my father ever helping out with the bills. My mother used to take all of her money from sewing and pay for the food or clothes or anything extra that we had in the house. She was probably pretty pissed off. My father was away quite often. When he came home to her there were always problems. My mother had nowhere to go with ten kids. My mother is a very strong person. She raised us all and put up with a lot from us. We were all trouble, all of us kids. We still are. To this day she is putting up with things from us. I never thought about why my mother didn't leave. We had ten kids. It's hard to pick up ten kids and just leave.

I didn't like my father too much for what he was doing. I still don't like him for that. Also he pushed us a lot. But I learned a lot from him too. We all worked for him. We cut wood for heat. We had our own garden. We always had some kind of job to do. He really pushed us a lot to work for him. As weird as it seems, he taught me a lot too, things like mechanics or keeping things clean. I learned those things. But I picked up something extra on the way.

I never really talked to my father about how he was treating my mother. I told him I was not happy with the way he dealt with things with my mother. I used to tell him how stupid he was for treating my mother that way. I think he is starting to mellow out a bit. He is not so physically violent. He doesn't hit her. But he still abuses her with his head. They have been together for forty years and they know how to get on each other's nerves now with just words, talking.

All of my brothers and me, we all had a time when it came pretty close about whether we were going to hit him back. We all had a period when we were just fed up with getting hit all the time. When you are being abused, you wonder: am I going to hit him back? I hated him when I was a kid. Nobody has ever struck him back, though. People have picked up things to hit him with and then held back. I just left home when I was sixteen instead. I never went back after I left.

I don't really remember anyone from when I grew up that was not violent. I grew up in school fighting with kids. It's just the way we grew up in that community. Where I grew up, everyone was fighting each other. I recall even my neighbours across the street who used to always be fighting outside, drinking and fighting with their wives. I used to babysit for my father's cousins when I was about ten years old and they used to come home at night drunk and start fighting. I used to see a lot of violence. I saw gun fights in the neighbourhood, with rifles and things. It was a small community. There was always a lot of police around, and a lot of violence. Prison was the same thing. Except you are locked into it. You can't get away from it.

When you grow up with family violence, you see that that is how anger is dealt with all the time. Whenever my mother was mouthing off at my father, he dealt with it by throwing something at her or he hit her. That just stayed in my subconscious. I never wanted to hit my wife. It was just automatic. I didn't plan it or want it to happen … it just happened like that.

Many times when I was watching my father beat my mother up, I told myself that I never wanted to do that when I got married. All my life until I left home, I said I never wanted to beat my wife. When I left home when I was sixteen, I thought that was the end of it. I even tried to fight with my brother before I got married because he was fighting with his wife. I picked up an ashtray and told him to stop it or I was going to hit him. I told him you are not supposed to beat up your wife if you love her. And then it ended up that I'm doing the same thing myself. I don't know why it happens.

Personally, I don't know how to control myself. I don't want to blame it on anybody else that I am beating up my wife. But I don't know why I do it. I never wanted to do it. But I just do it. It just happens like that. I have no control over it whatsoever. I can be so in love with my wife and love her so much and then all of a sudden something will start happening in the next few hours and it will start off in a big argument and I'll hit her. Things completely change for no reason and I don't know why. It probably doesn't even matter that it is her that I am beating. If it was another woman, the same thing would probably be happening.

My wedding night, I hit my wife. I still regret it to this day. On our wedding day she was getting pissed drunk and acting like an idiot. She was acting like a fool, and I hit her. I told her to smarten up, that everyone was watching us and that she was acting like a fool, getting pissed drunk and staggering around. I told her to straighten up. I still regret it. I would like to marry her again some day and just be sober and straight. Moments when you're supposed to be so happy, they turn out so wrong. It just makes me feel horrible. I never wanted things to happen like that.

My biggest problem ... I guess it has something to do with feeling that I have to be the man of the house. It's kind of intimidating for me to think that both the woman and man can be bosses of the house, equal. It always seemed like one or the other of us is the boss. That's the way I grew up. That is the way I learned it all my life. And that's the way that all of the people that I knew growing up acted. I've never really thought that we are going to be equal. I've said that we'll be equal. But I've never really thought that we would actually *be* equal. Being equal is something that I'm going to have to look at. We have a lot of problems with not communicating. That is probably a good reason why we don't communicate: because I always have the last say.

Women also engage in psychological abuse. It is just as hard on the guy to feel belittled and small and useless when your wife is making you feel small and making you feel useless. I know there are times that I thought I was doing pretty good. I look after my kids. I have a job. But still it feels like I get criticized by my wife all the time. Nothing is good enough.

I've seen other extremes as well, men whose wives treat them badly or their wives just left them. The men just put up with it. There are both extremes. I'm trying to find the middle ground now, finding a way to communicate.

Things have to be talked about when they come up. If you don't agree with the person, it's not enough to say: okay you're right, and walk away, because then it just builds up and builds up. You get saucier, and your wife gets saucier to you and then you explode. I never saw my parents negotiate. It wasn't always violence. But it would always be an argument and my father would win. My mother's ideas didn't matter. I think it would help to sit down and talk to my wife more openly. With my wife it is: Yes. No. See you later. There's no real talking. I don't understand it myself. We never talk about serious problems that we have.

When I am pissed off, I usually say: I'm leaving. She says: You're not going anywhere. She used to say: Are you going out to drink or to smoke drugs again? I would just say: I'm leaving. Perhaps it's better to say: I have to get out of here because I'm about to lose control. That's a better way of saying it than saying: I'm getting out of here, I'm fed up with your crap. Whenever I would say that she would say: No, you're not going out. But it's easy to think about saying these things in advance. When you're living it, it's a different thing. It's totally a change in lifestyle, to think about communicating openly. For me to be close to my wife … I want it to happen so bad. But I just can't imagine it. I just can't picture it, how it's going to be that we're talking to each other.

What I am finding about me going to healing circles is that just listening to women crying is helpful. Before if my wife would cry about things, I would tell her to shut up and stop crying. I would tell her that it's not going to help anything to cry. But she was probably crying sometimes for very valid reasons. I find that going to the healing circles and listening to women crying, I have discovered that there's another side to it. I always see a woman bitching at me. I never see what the man is doing. I never see what I am doing. It just seems so natural and normal to be giving your wife trouble again that you just do it. It seems so normal. You just do it when you don't even want to. It's just the way that we've communicated.

In the past, I haven't had much feeling for my wife about what her feelings or her problems are. I'm starting to try and think about why I have been beating on her, why she is always bitching at me, why she is accusing me of screwing around when I'm not doing it. Why are these problems happening? I need to start focusing on why these things are happening. Before I just accepted it and never tried to change anything. But it has gotten to the point where I see my kids crying and watching me fight with my wife. There is no alternative now. If I am going to stay with my wife either I change – change completely, stop the beating, stop the arguing – or just forget it.

I feel that just to say it's not going to work out and to just split is the easy way out. It's like suicide. It's like saying: we can't deal with the problem, we might as well split up. What will end up happening is that I'll end up with another woman and she'll end up with another guy and there will be two more groups that are doing the same thing, just spreading it around.

I need one or two years to know that I'm in control of my life, that we aren't arguing. Then there is a very good chance that I will talk to men. But I need to straighten my life out first. I would like some day to be able to talk to men, because I don't agree with that at all, men beating up on their wives or arguing all the time, or women arguing all the time. I don't like the fighting that happens around children. I worry for the men and women, but mostly why I worry is that my kids are seeing this all the time. Even if it's not hitting, it's arguing all the time. I'm not hitting my wife every day. Every blue moon I lose it. But every other day, we are arguing, and our kids see this all the time, and that's bad. My kids may end up in the exact same situation and they won't even know why it's happening. That's the way I feel: that I'm in this situation and I didn't place myself in it, it just happened, and I don't know why it's happening.

My plan now is to get my life on track. I see my own kids the way I saw myself. They are seeing the same thing: me beating on my wife, us arguing and fighting all the time … the drinking. My children are the ones that are hiding now, that are getting under the bed, not me. I'm just worried about what they are going to go through when they get older. I just want this to stop.

All of the men that I hang out with, they don't admit it, but they are having problems at home. I know that. I see it. It's obvious. But people try to pretend that they are not like that. In the back of my mind, I am thinking that that is a lie. I see their wife walking down the road every other day with a black eye and she claims to have fallen on a door knob or something. These people are drinking all the time and they still claim that they don't have problems. Men have to control themselves. Nobody deserves to get hit.

Lovers and
Healing Circles

INUIT WOMEN

Once the informant identified her or his "home region" (most of the infor-
mants were men; women took part in rather small numbers), the person was
asked to concentrate on any geographical feature for which a name was
remembered.   L. Müller-Wille, *Gazetteer of Inuit Place Names in Nunavik*[1]

Tucked away in brackets in this quote from the Inuit Place Names
Project is an intimation that the collection of maps in the last chapter
may be incomplete. Just as it is now recognized that Inuit place-name
maps reveal aspects of the land unimagined by Cartesian cartography,
there may be other perspectives on the world awaiting official recognition. There are at least two ways to read the silence of Inuit women.

On one reading, the homeland of all of the Inuit people of Québec is
circumscribed by the same boundaries. Soliciting the assistance of Inuit
women would only add more specificity to the lines already drawn. On
this reading not much, then, was left out of the place-names project by
the non-participation of women. Their contribution would have essentially enhanced the most significant opposition: that between Inuit and
Qallunaat cartographic history. This story ends more or less here.

On the other reading of the silence of Inuit women, their non-
participation in the place-naming project was not merely an accidental
but an essential characteristic of the enterprise. There is something about
the nature of Inuit women's daily lives that distinguishes it from the interests that go into place-naming projects and their attendant history. It is
an integral part of Inuit women's lives to stand in a different relationship

to things like boundaries and territory from their male counterparts. It is this second reading of the silence of Inuit women that I want to pursue.

On this second reading, place-naming maps reflect male uses of land and men's construction of an Inuit identity. The version of history that stands behind place-name maps does not embody the material conditions and preoccupations of all of Inuit society. In the first instance, the material conditions of life for men and women in traditional Inuit society were distinguished by a division of labour based on gender.[2] Male tasks included hunting, transportation, and using the umiak and kayak.[3] These tasks would have taken them to the limits of the boundaries delineated in the place-name maps. Women's tasks located women's daily lives within a different ambit.

The division of labour assigned to women the care of infants, their carrying and feeding, the preparation, cutting, and sewing of skins, the maintenance of oil lamps, food preparation, and cooking. Women also did small-scale hunting and fishing near the camp and collected plants, berries, algae, seafood, and eggs. If there had been place-naming maps made out of Inuit women's habitual exploitation of space, they would, for the most part, have been more contained. They would also have constituted a testament to a quite different web of natural, social, and historical relations. They would have served as an alternate record of how "the Inuit" organized space, rendered its aspects salient, and identified and ascribed value to its particular assets.

As with Inuit history generally, the transmission of Inuit women's history would not have been passed down through written texts. It might, indeed, infrequently have been recorded orally. The traces left by Inuit women's historical consciousness may have been more visceral than oral or written, embodied in dispositions. Just as Inuit men inscribed history in the naming of salient aspects of the physical space, Inuit women would have rehearsed a mnemonics consistent with their sphere of activity. So, for example, their history may have been inscribed on the early childhood of their children, impressed on the child by the particular formulas of inculcation that characterized Inuit domesticity. If a woman's particular history included abuse, that, similarly, would have been passed down, registering rapes and abductions in the quality of affection for the offspring, drawing out resignation on the next generation's early childhood.

Recollect that *Nuna* is the word for "land" in the Inupik and Upik dialects, suggesting at a generalized level "country." It is the territory

within which a man lives out his life and which is possessed by him.
Recollect that territorial claims recognize the presence of a system of
land use as evidence for delimiting the borders between Inuit and non-
Inuit jurisdictions. If the system of land use is based on how a man lives
out his life, then the boundaries of an Inuit homeland are men's boundaries. It is the space in which Inuit men feel at home. An Inuit woman's
homeland may overlap with, displace, and overspill these borders.

The fact that the primacy of male boundaries was legitimated by
place-naming reflects an asymmetry between men and women in both
Inuit society and in Qallunaat society, which generated the rules for
officialization. In the same way that the British and French assumed the
normality of acquiring territory beyond their realms, and in the same
way that the conventional cartographic enterprise assumed that territorial boundaries are not seasonally dependent, it is presumed that male
usages of space are the relevant ones for determining the limits of a
people's homeland. The tacitness of this assumption reflects women's
(Inuit and Qallunaat) relationship with power.

One interpretation of the legitimation of male conceptions of space
might pragmatically assert that the male boundaries are, as a matter of
cultural and historical fact, wider than women's boundaries, given the
geographically limited scope of women's usages. Male usages include
women's usages, whereas the inverse is not the case. Adopting male
usages is more generous in the ascription of territory to a people.

This interpretation, however, rests on a circular conception of what it
is to be a people, namely those who have historically populated *a given
territory*. Male use and occupancy only includes female use and occupancy where the relevant parameter is geographical and territorial.
Defending the integrity of a territorially defined people may be a more
remote priority for Inuit women. This may have to do with women's
experience at those boundaries given their distinctive practices within
them. Some of their experiences might render them ambivalent about
territorial definitions of peoplehood in a way that men's experiences
do not.

The division of labour that assigns to women the bearing of and caring
for children shapes their relationship to geographically defined peoplehood. Inuit women have been physically inseminated by "others"
throughout a long history of interactions across borders. From the Thule
amalgamation of the Dorset Inuit between 1000 and 1500 AD, through the
passage of any number of other "others" over the land – Viking, Siqinirmiut, Tarramiut, Itivimiut, Naskapi, Cree, whalers, traders, missionaries,

police, settlers, American and Canadian servicemen, construction workers, bureaucrats, American game hunters, eco-tourists, lawyers – Inuit
women have been much less implicated in warfare and negotiations
about territory than they have been in visceral entanglements and
impregnation.

The physicality of intercourse and pregnancy might well implicate
women differently than men in struggles between nations. The importance of nationality and peoplehood might feel different when the arena
for the merger of cultures is one's body. And the subsequent emotional
extension of this incubation – necessitated by the allocation of child-care
to women – might absorb women differently in agonistic histories. Inuit
women's history, one could say, has long suggested a more syncretic
understanding of culture. The result of the kind of contact Inuit women
often sustained with other groups did not suggest the death of some
homogeneous pre-contact culture but was frequently some form of
emotional or domestic involvement. Not infrequently, the result was a
child – a testament to the viability and tenacity of hybrids.

Women's practices, then, might not warrant the pseudo-pragmatic
Venn diagram that includes Inuit women's conception of peoplehood
within nominally wider male conceptions. Nunavik's homeland boundaries do not suggest an accidental (and thus incidental) conflation of
peoplehood with maleness. Geographically based definitions of a homeland are more integrally related to male preoccupations and practices. It
is easier for a man physically and culturally to absolve himself of the
messy emotional and political consequences of cross-border incubation
in order to re-perfect the impermeability of the interface.

A darker interpretation of the paramountcy of male conceptions of
space in defining nations and peoples has more to do with the position
of women *within* those male-defined boundaries. Something other than
the naive recognition that male use of geographical space is wider than
female explains why male usage is officialized. While the lesser relevance
of Inuit women's experience of space might have been reinforced by the
methodology of the place-names project and the demands of Qallunaat
officialization, it quite conceivably was also reinforced by a long local
history of the physical and emotional subjugation of Inuit women within
the space they shared with Inuit men. This subjugation would have
undermined women's authority in other domains.

This chapter's opening tales of violence likely recapitulate not only
cataclysmic social disruption at the Qallunaat/Inuit border. It is not
unreasonable to suggest that they speak to continuities pre-dating Inuit/

Qallunaat relations. It is conceivable that the woman beaten by a caribou leg and the man whose children cower under the bed tragically relived moments with a long and deep and largely invisible history. That this history may not have been recorded – orally or otherwise – speaks more to the public legitimacy allotted to Inuit women's historical consciousness than to its factual presence.

Gaps in the historical record can be inferred by the persistence of practices that take women's subjugation for granted as part of the backdrop for relations between women and men or between socially defined actors like husbands and wives. They can be inferred from the staggering regularity of similar tales,[4] or by peering between the lines of ethnographic accounts, if not by straightforwardly reading.

The following accounts can be found scattered all over the ethnographic record and are so frequently encountered as to lend credibility to the type of ahistorical generalizations anthropologists make about gender and kin relations in other cultures:

In 1905 a Netsilingmiut couple moved over to settle among the Asiagmiut, with their three grown sons. Of these sons, the eldest had an Asiagmiut wife. A local native declared he would have regular sexual intercourse with the woman. The husband did not want to acquiesce, but was not strong enough to prevent the aggressor, and in consequence, he speared his own wife so that the other could not have access to her.[5]

Sekrusuna had been a great one to tease poor Quanguaq ... He would taunt him by suggesting, when they were hunting together, that they go home to their "wife" now ... Sekrusuna also tantalized the poor man by promising him he might sleep with his wife when they returned, but whenever Quanguaq attempted to take advantage of this favor, he found the woman's lawful husband at her side. The husband thought this a great joke ... Besides all this, Sekrusuna beat his wife in order to demonstrate to Quanguaq the many advantages of being happily married. He beat her only when the widower was present.

One day in the spring ... Quanguaq drove his harpoon ... straight through the body of his friend Sekrusuna ... Quanguaq came home with both sledges and teams. He drove straight to the dead man's wife and told her that he was going to stay with her ... The widow meekly accepted her altered status.[6]

The behaviour of the men has a kind of stability to it. The ease of manoeuver by male protagonists lends a banality to the subjugation of women which speaks to its normalization in Inuit society.

Ethnographies also testify to the (at times) complete nullity of Inuit women's agency in matters of sexual and affinal choice. The irrelevance of women's individual desires and aspirations is tacit in the traditional understanding of adultery, which defines the latter in terms of the express or implied consent of the husband. If a husband consents to lend his wife to another man, the sexual liaison is legitimate. If a husband has not consented, then the act is adulterous and "can only be viewed as a challenge to his position as a man."[7] Rasmussen remarked on the effects of this effrontery amongst the Musk Ox Inuit in the 1920s. When he visited their societies he found that "all adult males in the fifteen families that made up the community in the early 1920s had been involved in a homicide, either as principals or accessories, and for each of them 'the motive was invariably some quarrel about a woman.'"[8] That Inuit men had a quasi-proprietary attitude to Inuit women can be inferred from how they reacted to any non-consensual physical intrusion on what they perceived to be within their sphere of control. How women felt about or construed the meaning of consent to sexual relations dwells in the shadows of ethnographic accounts.

Like the criteria for cartographic officialization that favours male land use, the parade of male anthropologists to the North generally perceived the world against the background of their own common sense. They normalized Inuit women's experience of violence against their assessment of non-Inuit women's experience of violence: something that does not stand in need of elaborate exposition or circumspect analysis. Hoebel, for example, offered an analysis of the violence surrounding sexual relations amongst the Inuit that suggested that the clearer demarcation of property rights in the Qallunaat institution of marriage would have precluded many such territorial disputes:

In part, the Eskimo difficulties are enhanced by the lack of marriage and divorce rituals which might demarcate the beginning and the end of a marital relationship. Marriage is entered into merely by bedding down with the intention of living together; divorce is effected simply by not living together any more … Shifts in marital status are so easy that an open invitation to home-breaking exists as a continuous temptation. Or put otherwise, there are no cultural devices signalizing marriage in such a way as to serve to keep out trespassers. This … reflects a lack of interest on the part of the Eskimo in stabilizing the family. It contributes to conflict by inviting intrusion. Things and wives are both easily borrowed and lent among the Eskimos, and in the case of wives there is a lack of clear demarcation of where borrowing ends and appropriation begins.[9]

The idea that the family could be stabilized around the metaphor of trespass (with the woman never the trespassee) lent banality to the parallel – and no less horrific – subjugation of Qallunaat women.

The failure to ask certain kinds of questions and make certain kinds of observations – a failure structured by the immersion of male anthropologists in their own society's practices – has thinned out the historical record. Rasmussen provides a good example of the partiality of male anthropologists and the concomitant marginalization of Inuit women's voices in his response to a Caribou Eskimo case: "Igjugarjuk, a headman of Padlermiut, was rebuffed by the parents of a girl he sought as his wife. To have his way and to show his pride he lay in ambush by the door of her family's hut, shooting down the father, mother, brothers and sisters, seven or eight in all, until only the girl survived, whereupon he took her to wife."[10] Rasmussen, we are told, knew this man and considered him "clever, independent, intelligent, and a man of great authority among his fellows."

And the woman? How does she feel going off with a man who has just murdered her family, her personal history, the people who embodied all of her early memories? What did this event mean to her? These questions were not part of the record of the event. Rasmussen – as with those of us who find the silence of Inuit women's voices eerie – was inescapably conditioned by his own historicity. His failure, or inability, to ask certain questions created a moral climate in which Inuit women's perspectives were pushed to the margins. The limits of his imagination *reinforced* the normality of the asymmetry between men and women. By reinforcing this normality, he was unavoidably constituting the community, not merely reflecting it.

In both Qallunaat and Inuit societies, the ordinary worlds of men and women were not coextensive. Speculation about the sensibilities of women is necessitated by the officialization, in maps and ethnography, of the male use and occupation of space. The place where the Inuit feel at home, feel that the world is familiar, may not be contiguous for men and women. Inuit women – like Qallunaat women – may indeed feel that they are not at all at home in the space that Inuit men have carved out for themselves. Women's history would make topographical reference to all of the familiar places where the particularity of women's experiences are daily played out.

This transcultural, and less territorial, women's history, however, would not be precisely coextensive with Inuit women's history either. Inuit women also moved with their partners over the land, in seasonal hunting patterns or into the sedentary camps around the Hudson's Bay Company posts. This is an Inuit woman's occupation of the land as much as an Inuit man's; there are overlaps in usage. Inuit men have also participated in their mother's domesticity through the experiences of early childhood. They may, as the second tale above intimates, identify with her misery. The domestic space is shared by both mother and child, male and female.

Sometimes participating in one practice means that one cannot fully participate in another. This may be because of the material demands of the practice, as with the incompatibility of hunting and trapping/trading economies. But it may also be because the intelligibility of one practice conflicts with the intelligibility of another. The ways of understanding one practice make it difficult to grasp the ways of understanding another.

Nitya Duclos alludes to this when she remarks that outsider feminists have difficulty understanding tensions between the historical consciousness of Native women and Native men. Qallunaat women have difficulty conceiving the issue as other than a struggle between women's rights and cultural autonomy. For outsider women, the former trumps the latter with its presumptive moral weight.[11] However, Inuit women's perception of Inuit men will be conditioned by their participation in both Inuit history and women's history in ways that Qallunaat women's perception of Inuit men will not.

Belonging shapes understanding. Qallunaat who wish to understand the Inuit sense of the land, linked to the latter's bodies and carried with them wherever they go, need the intellectual device of a place-name map as an intermediary. Similarly, men who aspire to see the world beyond the horizon of their gender must force into their minds a set of experiences that women carry with themselves in their bones. This situation gives rise to questions about what it is to belong to a group.

Inuit women's distinctive experience of Inuitness indicates that while historical events can be grouped under the category of culture, there is a diversity of experience within – and overspilling – that grouping. Just as the opposition between Inuit and Qallunaat history in the first chapter suggested new possibilities for historiography, looking for the probable experiences of individual human beings under categories such as age, social status, physical ability, or gender might provide challenges to the official delimitation of the group. As well, the life experiences of individual members may be at odds with some or many of such probable and predictable group experiences.

Being Inuit or being an Inuit woman is not a matter of being one set
of determinative things. The rest of this chapter examines more closely
the concept of identity and the group-determining ways in which it is
constituted. I also take up an issue intimated in the last chapter but left
largely unexplored – the issue of agency. More particularly I explore the
dimensions of agency in situations where force aims to bend the wills of
those it wishes to subjugate.

In the discussion of the history of the Inuit and Qallunaat in Nunavik,
I offered a counter to the idea that a continuously subjugated people
progressively disappears over time by incorporating the will of the
oppressor into their daily actions. There is an implication in this equa-
tion of the self with will that subjugated people have a reduced scope for
self-expression, and hence for moral action. Wittgenstein's analogy of
the river and riverbed was drawn upon as a way to look at elements of
reciprocity and historical development in these types of encounters. The
analogy suggests, however, a naturalness to the asymmetry of power
between the two peoples, an overall give and take in situations of subjugation. This aura of co-determination does not resonate with the way
that force is experienced. It does not, for example, accurately reflect the
position of the Inuit left destitute around deserted HBC trading posts
after the company bought out Révillon Frères in 1936.

The dilemma of agency in situations of oppression could be explored
using the particularities of Qallunaat and Inuit experiences, or the social
experiences of the young and old, or impoverished and comfortable, or
any of several asymmetrical social oppositions. In the following material,
however, I focus on the grammar of intimacy between men and women.
The children cowering under the bed in violent homes alert us that this
is a telling opposition for the delivery of justice in Nunavik. This focus
on family violence is another account of the world to which an agent of
justice – as well as anyone who felt for those children – would give
judicial notice.

A further element alluded to in the last chapter is the possibility for
communication across group-determined experiences. In the light of
ethnocentric cartography, in light of European decisions to determine
title to North American land on the basis of discovery and possession –
despite the pre-existence of an indigenous people on the land – or in
light of self-interested economies and political agendas, what might be
the possibilities for rendering incommensurable frames of reference
commensurable? What are the possibilities for beholding the particular

expression of humanity of another human being, despite how perception is predisposed by the practices of the groups in which we find ourselves?

This emphasis on communication suggests that the faculties of perception and attention are vital to an understanding of the self and the other. Our perplexity about justice is aroused by the odd, allusive, and sometimes jarring configuration of particular cases; and it is to those scenarios that I now turn in investigating the grammar of identity and intimacy.

BELONGING

Two adoption cases heard in the Supreme Court of Canada in the last twenty years raise questions of Solomonic proportions about what it is to be an Aboriginal person. The first case is *Natural Parents* v. *The Superintendent of Child Welfare et al.* The second is *Racine* v. *Woods.*[12]

In the first case, a male child, the son of registered members of an Indian band, was admitted to hospital at age of seven weeks in a condition near death as a result of injury and neglect. The child's life was preserved by a hospital nurse, petitioner in the case at bar. The child was discharged into her care on a foster-care basis. The child remained with this woman and her family except for a brief stay with his blood parents at age three that resulted in another episode requiring a stay in the hospital. The foster parents subsequently applied to adopt the child, which the trial judge described as "now a member of the family in every way but blood relationship." The legal issue in the case at the Supreme Court level was whether the provincial Adoption Act conflicted with the Indian Act.

Section 10 (1) of the Adoption Act states that "*For all purposes* an adopted child becomes upon adoption the child of the adopting parent, and the adopting parent becomes the parent of the child, as if the child had been born to that parent in lawful wedlock." Section 11 (1) (d) of the (pre-C-31) Indian Act designates an Indian for the purposes of the Indian Act as "the legitimate child of a male person who is a member of a band or is the legitimate child of a male person who is a direct descendant in the male line of a male person who is a member of a band." It was held, in this case, that the two provisions were not inconsistent. While other adopted children lose all legal filiation with their blood parents, an Indian child remains an "Indian" despite an adoption that would otherwise obliterate all ties to blood parents, to culture, to community.

This decision appears to suggest that, at least for the purposes of the Indian Act, an Indian can be defined purely by blood. It implies that Indians by birth remain Indians for life even while contemplating the possibility that such individuals may never know about their culture, their history, their language, their people, their community, or any of the other criteria intuitively embraced by our understanding of "Indianness." Indeed, it contemplates the proposition that, whether Indians by birth recognize it or not, they are still Indian. In this sense, Indians are born and not made. A child is an Indian despite himself.

In the case of *Racine*, a female child, Leticia, was born to full-status Indians. The blood mother of the child, by her own admission, had a serious alcohol problem. When the child was six weeks old, she was apprehended by the Children's Aid Society and five months later was placed in the foster care of the plaintiffs, one of whom was non-Native and the other Métis. Over the years the birth mother made a number of sporadic efforts to retrieve her child and have her cared for by a family member; however, it was not until the child was six years old that the mother made an application for *habeas corpus*. At that time the plaintiffs submitted an application for *de facto* adoption which became the issue in the case. An attempt was made to determine the best interests of the child in settling where her home would be.

It was part of the birth mother's argument that it is a constituent element of the best interests of the child that she not be cut off from her Indian heritage and culture, something the finality of an adoption order necessitates. It was the contention of the adoptive parents and the Supreme Court that, important a factor as her Indian heritage and culture might be, the duration and strength of her attachment to the Racines was more important. The significance of belonging to a culture and heritage that preserves cultural integrity as opposed to belonging to a family that preserves emotional integrity abates over time.

Of course, Leticia does not choose her emotional attachment to her adoptive family either. This is something that fate has had a hand in bringing about. Her adoptive mother was there, present to her. Similarly, she cannot now simply choose to care more about her birth mother. Her alienation from her blood mother is something that circumstance has made *almost* inevitable; "almost," because she may still choose to *develop* a relationship with her mother as an adult, driven by the not negligible bond of blood. She is more likely to feel a longing for intimacy with her birth mother than a sense of intimacy. A sense of intimacy is not likely to be something she will feel, despite herself.

What is being weighed in this case is a form of attachment that outweighs the need for attachment to community and cultural identity; it stands as a prerequisite for the robust acquisition of cultural identity. Neither option is a matter of choice for Leticia. As is emphasized throughout the court levels, however, bonding to a family does not eradicate the need for cultural identification with the culture into which one is born by blood. Belonging to a family does not satisfy the need to belong to a culture or community.

Madame Justice Wilson noted that "Hall JA did not underestimate the importance of the fact that the child was an Indian. However, he adopted the conclusion the trial judge drew from the expert evidence before her as to the Racines' sensitivity to the interracial aspect and their appreciation of the need to encourage and develop in Leticia a sense of her own worth and dignity and the worth and dignity of her people. The trial judge found that they had amply displayed their ability to guide Leticia through any identity crisis she might face in her teenage years."[13] The courts do not question that Leticia is an Indian by blood and that this fact is crucial for a complete understanding of *who she is*. In this case, however, her Indianness, though inherent in her blood, is something that will need to be learned at a later age, almost as one learns a foreign language. Perhaps even more incongruous, her coming to terms with her "Indianness" is something that will be facilitated by adults who are in fact foreigners to her culture and identity. Is culture something that can be learned as one learns a foreign language? Can culture be mediated by people who, sympathetic as they might be, are not members of that culture? Can non-Native people help an Aboriginal person understand what it means to be Native? Can a non-Native and a Métis adult help a child understand what it means to be an Inuk? Can they help her understand what it means to be a Cree if they never bring her to the land where the Cree live? If she never speaks to a Cree person herself? Can they help a child understand what it means to be a Mohawk of Akwasasne, as opposed to a Mohawk of Kahnawake? Can they help her understand what it means to grow up as an Akwasasne Mohawk if she does not spend any of her childhood growing up on Akwasasne? Could they help her to understand what it meant to be a Beothuk if she were the last surviving Beothuk?

If Leticia must learn *who she is* as an adolescent, then what does it mean to say that she is an Indian by birth? In what sense can they help her learn any more than what it is to be marked by blood as an Indian, to be born of a status-Indian mother who had severe alcohol problems, to be born of an alcoholic Indian mother who abandoned her to be brought up by Métis and non-Native parents? In what sense can they help her to do any more than to love herself *despite* who she is? Surely the *most* they can do is to help her to love herself *because* of who she is: an Indian by birth, whose alcoholic status-Indian mother abandoned her at birth, who has lived to tell the tale. In the process of coming to love herself *because* of who she is, will she not need to love herself *despite* what her adoptive mother's people have done to her blood mother's people? That is, despite who her adoptive mother is? That is, despite who she is?

Both of these cases raise a plethora of questions about Native identity and the preservation of the emotional, moral, and cultural integrity of human beings. It is often felt that a definition of Indianness based on blood raises any number of troubling implications. It generates intimations of tribalism, of eugenics. When referencing membership to the contingency of birth, one hears echoes of such invidious expressions as "pure blood," "half-breed," and "pedigree." In the face of the ominous implications of rooting culture in something as involuntary as blood, we flee to a notion of culture based on something less fatalistic, something under the control of human agents.

Without denying that the Racines may well be the best placed in the circumstances to help Leticia negotiate her identity as an adolescent, I would contend that we understand this scenario to be a troubling compromise precisely because it is part of the nature of culture that it often *is* rooted in something that is involuntary, that cannot be taught at a later age, that is rooted in blood, in the circumstances of our birth, and in fate.

In light of this understanding of culture as something that cannot be manipulated without limit, the choices presented to the court in deliberating the best interests of the child are Solomonic and speak to a deeper human tragedy underlying the options. Either option divides the child. The metaphor of blood in fact evokes a deep undercurrent of the notion of culture, even though it brings us into very troubled waters, often darkly coloured by tragedy and grief. Blood evokes the inescapable elements of culture.

Leticia's dilemma is echoed in a haunting passage quoted in Erik Erikson's *Identity, Youth and Crisis*: "'My God,' a Negro woman student exclaimed ... 'what am I supposed to be integrated *out of*? I laugh like my grandmother – and I would rather die than not laugh like her.'"[14] Erik Erikson goes on to describe the impact of this statement on other black students who heard the remark: "There was silence in which you could hear the stereotypes click, for even laughter has now joined those aspects of Negro culture and Negro personality which have become suspect as the marks of submission and fatalism, delusions and escape." It would appear that to embrace who you are is to embrace a description of yourself over which you have no control.

For people who have been abused or silenced it appears that the world into which one is born has the power to define you, it ascribes to you who you are, and it describes you as a subjugated, humiliated person. It appears able to obliterate your humanity. So little room seems left to create a counter-interpretation that if you do not embrace the self the world imposes on you, you are almost embracing a non-entity, something vaporous and insubstantial, a false reality, mere ephemera. Not to laugh the way that your grandmother laughed is to have an artificial laugh – or to be without laughter altogether – because an alternative grandmother did not exist.

In her novel *Beloved* Toni Morrison creates this sense of the implosion of self-understanding under the weight of a dreadful force. She tells the story of an ex-slave in America, Sethe, who, under unspeakable duress, murders her daughter rather than have her beloved child taken back South under the authority of the Fugitive Bill to endure the harm that she herself lived through. Several of the characters – including the murdered child's grandmother who was a witness to the murder, a man who was a slave on the same farm as Sethe, the child's sister who was spared, by moments, the same fate, and Sethe herself – try to come to terms with this event. The understandings range from characterizing the mother's behaviour as animal ("You got two feet, Sethe, not four") to decrying that "anybody white could take your whole self for anything that came to mind. Not just work, kill, or maim you, but dirty you. Dirty you so bad you couldn't like yourself anymore. Dirty you so bad you forgot who you were and couldn't think it up."[15] The crushing force of oppression sometimes feels powerful enough to push into the most intimate reaches of self-understanding and motivation.

Erickson describes the despair of recognizing that the world has constructed a negative identity for you in the African-American context:

[W]hat if there is nothing in the hopes of generations past nor in the accessible resources of the contemporary community which would help to overcome the negative image held up to a minority by the "compact majority"? Then, so it seems, the creative individual must accept the negative identity as the very base line of recovery. And so we have in our American Negro writers the almost ritualized affirmation of "inaudibility," "invisibility," "namelessness," "faceless-ness," – a "void of faceless faces, of soundless voices lying outside history," as Ralph Ellison puts it.[16]

We cannot hear soundless voices that lie outside of history. We can imagine now what someone who was never asked to speak might have said. We can imagine now what *we* might have said, but it is nonsensical to hear something that is inherently inaudible. Of course Ellison is not asking us to do so; he is invoking the image as a literary device.

The image of voices lying outside of history draws attention to the way that force maintains a deafness to counter-histories. Resisting this imag-ery of the implosion of identity under the force of more powerful public ascriptions does not, however, necessitate a flight to an understanding of the self as something internally and freely generated, a wholly private understanding, nor to conclusions about an axiomatic solipsism between cultures.

Analogous to the manner in which we are moved by the literary image of a "void of faceless faces, of soundless voices lying outside history," we are seduced by the philosophical image of a private language, a world of meaning existing outside the public sphere of meaning, as if such a thing were possible or even conceivable. We are also often tempted to create similar images about morality, about culture, and about identity: that these are merely private things which have meaning only insofar as we confer meaning upon them, that these are purely internal constructions. We are seduced by the image of fundamental non-communication between individual human beings and fundamental and pervasive mis-communication across culturally determined worlds of meaning. There is an analogy between solipsism and relativism. It seems that both are conceivable.

Wittgenstein has done much to highlight the meaninglessness of this conception of a private language. In *Philosophical Investigations* he focuses on what it means to learn a language and what it means to learn a mother tongue as opposed to a second language. He alludes to the seduction of privately constructed languages with reference to St Augus-tine: "And now, I think, we can say: Augustine describes the learning of human language as if the child came into a strange country and did not understand the language of the country; that is, as if it already had a language, only not this one. Or again: as if the child could already *think*, only not yet speak. And 'think' would here mean something like 'talk to itself.'"[17] It is the latter image, of a child being in possession of a prior language, that we find so alluring. We imagine we can hear a mother tongue as if it too had the odd musical qualities of another language, as if it were cacophony of symbols, not yet hinged to meaning. We think we are doing something or saying something meaningful when we imagine in this way, forgetting that we have used our mother tongue to articulate the image, forgetting that we are articulating the image to another speaker of our mother tongue.

We move into other cultures and are similarly provoked with a sense that we might be able to perceive of our own as if we were complete foreigners to it. We imagine that we must be able to conceive of a pre-cultural, pre-moral, pre-linguistic vantage point which characterizes reality outside of the characterizations of known languages. We are seduced by the image of "translating from reality" into English in the same way that we translate from English into French. This seduction is often provoked when we see the crumbling of highly cherished world views that used to make more or less comprehensive sense of human life. We search for safeguards against the future possibility of such fragility. An ironic or relativistic stance towards all of one's own commitments and attachments, even the deepest, seems to provide such a security; but this kind of general prophylactic is neither effective nor meaningful. This can be illustrated by way of the following pair of scenarios.

When Toby Morantz says that Indians originally used to regard missionaries as a form of bingo, as a form of entertainment, we chuckle to ourselves.[18] Those of us of European derivation can be delighted at this image, recognizing that our first emissaries must have appeared odd, even quaint, in their stubborn sincerity. We are tempted by our sense of delight to imagine that we might be capable of laughing at ourselves today, that we might have a similar omnipotent distance from ourselves, that we could see our own earnest preoccupations as a form of entertainment.

Laughing at ourselves while perceiving missionaries as a form of bingo is a valid move away from ethnocentrism. This strange-making manoeuver does not, however, justify the speculation that perhaps all of our beliefs are suspendable and that even our most cherished and core beliefs may be "mere" cultural and historical artifacts. Just as there is a logical impossibility in formulating the private-language argument, there is a logical impossibility in formulating a radical relativism, a failure to recognize that this ironical stance is a move to a more sophisticated cultural and historical position.

The shallowness of this position can be illustrated by the 1991 apology of the Oblates for the physical and sexual abuses their religious order inflicted upon Native people in residential schools. It is hard to see this apology, by analogy with the missionaries-as-bingo example, as entertaining. It is hardly possible to claim that the Oblates were being duped by the popular sentiment of the times, blindly conforming to today's common sense. We feel that those amongst us who laugh at the Oblates are simply crass, that the scoffers must not really understand what is going on. If they did, they could not react in such a manner.

For those of us who are non-Indian, in order to get sufficient historical or cultural distance to find the early missionaries silly, we have to already have taken very seriously regrets about the lamentable ways that Native people were treated by Europeans; we have to have absorbed some history as *history* and not as cultural artifact. In seeing the early missionaries as a form of public entertainment, the listener is invited to see the history from the point of view of another party to it. Enough of this understanding of history has been translated that most of us can "get" it in the 1990s.

The difficulty in seeing things from no particular point of view at all is *not* just because it makes us uncomfortable (in which case the relativist can ask us to try to get over our squeamishness) but because it cannot intelligibly be done. One cannot adopt this stance and perceive *any* of the salience of the world. Things only look like cultural or historical artifacts from the inside of another culture and from another moment in time. Similarly, in the realm of attachments to the world, there is no way of maintaining aloofness from the world that is not also a way of being in the world, a way of making daily rearrangements with its contingencies and demands.

Clearly this does not mean that *none* of our deepest sentiments and attachments is a sham. Scepticism is only meaningful, however, against a backdrop of things that are taken for granted. Wittgenstein makes this point with respect to the grammar of doubt.

Doubts, Wittgenstein points out, belong within a world of accepted meaning. To doubt something is to accept certain things groundlessly, without explanation. Descartes's universal doubt, for example, cannot do what he believes it can do – suspend the veracity of everything – as he must at least take for granted that the word "doubt" has the meaning he assumes it has in order for his exercise to proceed. It is an empirical fact that words have the meaning they have. Doubt comes to birth in a world that is already ordered.

Wittgenstein invites us to imagine a pupil who will not let his teacher explain anything to him, because he constantly interrupts with doubts about the existence of things, the meaning of words, etc. The teacher replies: "Stop interrupting me and do as I tell you. So far your doubts don't make sense at all." The teacher's impatience is justified, because the pupil's doubt is hollow. His questions are not really legitimate questions. He has not learnt how to ask questions; he has not learned the practice that he is being taught. Not calling things into doubt is often a prerequisite for learning certain activities. The child learns by believing the adult, and doubt comes *after* belief.[19] Learning a game means that we can be corrected, that we can be wrong, that we may be making a mistake. We look to our teachers when we are uncertain. If we are learning a game, we do not simply make up new rules when we do not know how to go on.

Similarly, we are constrained from arbitrarily doubting our deepest regrets because of the way the concept of doubt functions: we are taught the *appropriate* parameters of doubt. We doubt when there is a reason to doubt. Subsequent history, the protests of Natives, and closer scrutiny of Native/non-Native relations has given us ample reason to reflect on the rightness of what the early missionaries did.

In the case of ethnocentrism and racism, particular accounts and grievances from other peoples – or more corporeally, ways that the other flinches from certain reactions and responds warmly to others – provide the signposts about how to continue. This is not a turning away from the particularity of the world to the aloof stance of scepticism and relativism; it is rather an immersion in its bewildering multiplicity and complexity. This order of attention sets out the possibilities for remaining open to counter-interpretations and a counter-hegemonic history. More attention to historical particulars will generate its own grounded form of relevant scepticism, will show one how to go on, point out where and in exactly what way continuing in a particular direction would be ethnocentric. This requires caring passionately about getting it right rather than declining *all* of the potentially suspect commitments that pull one in different directions.

This understanding that there are public constraints already set on what it means to be doubting – that we cannot manipulate the meaning of things without limit – has implications for understanding agency. One does not advance in one's understanding of other human beings by a sheer internal stance of scepticism or irony; what is required is attention to a world that is set beyond our wills. But similarly, understanding ourselves requires attending to things that have been set before we turn our attention to them. We learn, as well, the appropriate construal of our behaviour.

We may be able to make sense of what it means for Leticia to discover who she is when it is framed this way. There is a story being told about her, whether she recognizes it or not. She is not completely at home in the world until she knows the truth about herself. She may be deluded in feeling at home in the world, superficially familiar with herself.

Because we are born into a world that is already ordered, part of recovering our memory is recovering a collective memory. This is part of the identity that an adolescent Indian who has been adopted out will have to recover. For an Aboriginal person to retain Aboriginal status means far more than retaining eligibility for tax exemptions and free post-secondary education under the Indian Act. It also means retaining Aboriginal status to keep intact the possibility of discovering who one is.

Not only do we discover the story that is being told about us from the moment of our birth, we discover a story that began long before our birth. Just as we can recollect our individual history wrongly, we can also be ignorant of the history of our people; we can think we have the facts and the best characterization but be wrong. Hence those among us who went through secondary schools in the Maritimes and never learned that the Mi'kmaq were hunted and shot by Europeans do not really know our history, do not really know our culture, do not really possess an accurate characterization of our people. The Mi'kmaq know more about us than we know ourselves.

When we talk about race being defined by blood, as the adoption cases intimate, it is not blood in the geneticist's sense, or the government's sense of the double-mother rule: it is blood in the poetic or spiritual sense of the moment of our birth placing a stamp of fate on us that is as much a fact of the world as the genetic imprint in our blood. History culminates in the circumstances of our birth.

The fact that Leticia's people have been so badly abused and demoralized must be taken into account when she discovers that her Indian mother is abusive or alcoholic: this is not *just* an individual choice on her mother's part. The fact that Leticia and other Native children were taken away from their families in part defines an Indian child, born to a status Indian mother in Portage la Prairie, Manitoba, September 4. Part of the ordering of the world into which Leticia is born is that her people have been so badly demoralized that some of them cannot take care of their children. Part of this demoralization comes from the fact that

Leticia's mother's people have had their children taken away from them purely because they were Indian and not because of any individual choices about caring for their children.

This recollection in Native people's blood of what happened in residential schools was eloquently told by William Elm, an Oneida elder: "Our parents, our grandparents, were taken there. Their traditions were ripped away. Language was ripped away. Motherhood was ripped away. Fatherhood was ripped away. There were no role models for our grandmothers, our grandfathers, or our fathers and mothers. My parents were in residential schools. They came out of there not knowing anything about being a parent, not knowing how to show affection, not knowing what a grandmother's hug was like … and they passed that on to their children and to me."[20] If we are Indian, then in our blood is this inherent memory.

Though we may find ourselves completely alone, we carry our family, our community, and our culture within us. This is so whether we recognize it or not. An Ojibway elder, who insists on being allowed to heal his people who are in prison, talked about this recognition: "I listened to a psychologist who was part of a team that was hired by the prison system to look into why so many Native women had committed suicide. He could not understand why Native women were destroying themselves. It had become a terrible crisis within the prison. I said to him, 'In part it is happening because these women have been abused. It is an inherent memory of the hundreds of years of abuse that have been done to us. They have lived with the hopelessness that so many of our people have lived with. They have given up. The only way that those women see out is to die.'"[21] Regardless of what we do with the pain that our families inflict upon us, we can never become any less their children.

Because we cannot escape the story that has been told about us and that is being told about us, part of learning to be at home in the world is coming to terms with who we are, apart from who we would wish ourselves to be. This is a restorative process. It is not necessarily filled only with grief: we can recover our grandmother's laugh at the same time as we recover her bitterness. And although history culminates in the circumstances of our birth, history is multiplex and manifold, contested and reinterpreted. The voices of a counter-history or a counter-literature can be strong and vibrant – even in circumstances where all that is left is a cry of grief. And these voices are capable of wearing opposition down with the power of their accounts. Erickson talks about the restorative nature of these counter-histories:

In a haunting way they [the black authors cited] defend a latently existing but in some ways voiceless identity against the stereotypes which hide it. They are involved in a battle to reconquer for their people, but first of all … for themselves, what Vann Woodward calls a "surrendered identity." I like this term because it does not assume total absence, as many contemporary writings do – something to be searched for and found, to be granted or given, to be created or fabricated – but something to be recovered. This must be emphasized because what is latent can become a living actuality, and thus a bridge from past to future.[22]

Recovering a surrendered identity is a vital part of learning how to speak, locating ourselves behind our words.

At the very heart of this restorative process is a conception of individual human beings who are attempting to speak on their own behalf. It is the emphatic affirmation of the humanity of the individual that creates an urgency to the individual's quest: something vitally human may be lost. This is a conception of the individual that is infused with a collective identity but not wholly captured by it. The emphasis on cultural identity is a powerful demand to be "heard and seen, recognized and faced as *individuals with a choice* rather than as men marked by what is all too superficially visible."[23]

The same may be said of blood. Biology is not a final destiny for human beings as it is a paradigmatically human capacity to understand the meaning of our destiny and to decide what we will do with it. Only human beings have a choice between resisting our destiny and coming to terms with it, between feeling at the mercy of and at peace with particulars.

Thus far I have dealt with how our participation in various collectivities shapes our identities and how there are elements of identity that are beyond the will of the individual. Identity – collective or individual – is not simply an internal, privately determined phenomenon. I cannot make of myself whatever I want, not only because of material constraints on my behaviour but because I do not single-handedly create the meaning of my behaviour but rather come to understand it.

But neither does identity reduce to a mere collage of publicly ascribed significations. While agency is constrained by the world in which it must operate, it is not determined by it. I have alluded to the possibilities for collective counter-interpretations of history in the context of oppression. I want now to examine in more detail the possibilities for the expression of agency, particularly in the context of force, and in the context of understanding and intimacy.

THE STORY IN THE SOUL OF THE LOVER

Children must have been the attentive recipients of a language before their doubts are any more than posturing or before they are able to ask the right questions – questions that mean something in the subject studied. But when a child has learned how to ask questions she will not just be proceeding in parrotlike fashion: she will transcend the practice in which her questions arise, forcing it to respond to her idiosyncratic needs. Sometimes questioning can push the practice in new directions, extending the boundaries of the subject altogether. What Simone Weil said about mathematics is true of questions and of identity: "a collective cannot so much as add together two and two: only an individual mind can do that."[24]

It is also of the nature of identity-formation to be a characteristically personal enterprise. If Leticia searches for her past by having her horoscope done or by watching westerns, this says something different about her than if she tracks down her half-sister. While it is of the essence of our moral decisions that they are objective – that we can be mistaken about how we have characterized our behaviour – it is simultaneously of the essence of our moral decisions that they are subjective, that they are stamped with our personal imprimatur. It is of the essence of our moral decisions that we are alone when we make them. I believe that this is what a Native activist, who had spent many years in a federal penitentiary, was getting at when he responded with anger to two younger Native ex-prisoners who were complaining about the misery that they had seen in prison. After listening to them talk, he said:

When I hit death row there was no place to go but up. You [other ex-prisoners] are talking about all of the things that happened on the inside ... I have seen the things that you are talking about. I have seen guys get stabbed. I have seen them get killed. I have seen them hang themselves. I have seen them carried out. I know about the suffering that prisoners go through. But I want to bring in the other side too, because when I was on death row, I had to ask myself, "Well, where does the responsibility lie? Nobody is in here with me anymore. I cannot blame anybody." I had to look at my own self.[25]

These words speak volumes about the activist. His reaction reveals who he is. A different man would have reacted differently to what he saw; at the same time, his reaction reveals to us the kind of man he is.

The highly particularistic style of literature conveys the central importance of the idiosyncrasy of character, the non-generalizable truths of individual lives, the things that if said or done by a different person would not mean the same thing, the unpredictable ways that individual response to events reveals the content of character. So, for example, in Morrison's *Beloved*, it was the man who had been similarly harmed as a slave, a childhood friend of Sethe, who refused to accept the necessity in her act of murder. Who else could level so horrible a judgment ("You got two feet, Sethe, not four") and still be a sympathetic character? The clicking tongues of the white society that sent her to jail for her crime were whispering similar things, but their judgments read like the ugly and ignorant perpetuation of racial injustice. The non-generalizable manifestations of character – who says what and how, and how the sometimes-tormented particularities of response to events reveal who one is – this order of specificity matters in characterizing moral actions.

This non-generalizable, non-collectively determined response to the world characterizes our sense of identity. We resist, even within ourselves, the eradication of our individual humanity that comes from defining ourselves by the contingencies of our birth. What renders us invisible as human beings is being "marked by what is all too superficially visible" and not "recognized and faced as individuals with a choice." We will come to understand the magnitude of what we have done to Leticia by hearing her story, by seeing how she comes to terms with being by blood an Indian whose alcoholic status Indian mother abandoned her so that she was brought up by Métis and non-Native parents. Perhaps it is not quite so serious as we might have thought. Perhaps it is more tragic than any of us could have imagined. Only Leticia can tell us. This is true even though Leticia herself may not be able to find the words to tell us. This is true even if Leticia herself has not yet got a handle on her story and what she says rings hollow. This is true even if Leticia is no longer alive. And these things are true because although it is Leticia's story, her story also belongs to the world. In belonging to the world, it belongs to only one individual born into an unreproducible time and space.

What does it mean then, that we can understand another human being's story when both that person and we ourselves are shaped by our background, when background shapes understanding, when our understanding of the world depends on the culture and language and time into which we are born? Because we have come to birth in a world that is ordered, understanding requires a form of attentiveness to the world to make sure that what we are hearing is the other person's story and not merely echoes of our own. It requires attention to our own humanity to make sure that our reactions to the world are not mediated by inherent memories of abuse or those aspects of our culture and personality that are "suspect as the marks of submission and fatalism, delusions and escape." For those of us who have not been subjugated or abused, it requires attention to ensure that our reactions to the world are not clouded by a sense of belonging to our privilege.

Simone Weil talked of this latter obstacle when she insisted that the cry of one who believes that he or she is being harmed – in a sense of "harm" that implies injustice – is a "silent" cry. Peter Winch's struggle to understand this formulation is worth citing at length:

[T]here are special obstacles *in the soul of the reader* in the way of recognizing protests at real injustice. "Attention" is necessary; and the peculiar difficulty of my attending to someone in such a situation is that it requires me to understand that we are both equal members of a natural order which can at any time bring about such a violation of whoever it may be, including myself. That is, I cannot understand the other's affliction from the point of view of my own privileged position; I have rather to understand *myself* from the standpoint of *the other's* affliction, to understand that my privileged position is not part of my essential nature, but an accident of fate.[26]

The sense of merit that attaches itself to privilege is often more deeply lodged in the bone than the marks of submission; the former disguises an interest in appearing natural.

To understand the affliction of others, we must understand who they are in their context and in their detail, in the accidents of their fate. This is not an impossible task. We do not have to hear every fact about them, only the facts that are relevant to their story. The relevant details may be breathtakingly brief. The relevant facts may not even approach words. In a fabric store on Avenue du Parc in Montréal, they may be a series of numbers tattooed into an arm. They may dwell in the way someone holds her spine. I am reminded in this context of a woman in a Native healing circle who addressed the circle in her turn:

"My name is X. I want to talk about what has happened to me ... but every time I have tried to tell my story, I have not been able to get past the first sentence. This time I am going to try and tell my story."

She took a deep breath and continued.

"I was put in a residential school as a child ... "

At this point, she broke down weeping. She wept for a long time, unable to put words to anything more than that.[27]

Without an exhaustive compendium of the facts of this woman's life, it is not inconceivable that some might respond by saying that they understand what she is talking about. Some in the circle may respond with an immediacy that shows us they understand exactly what she is talking about. This response may be without words. She may be speaking in the plaintive hope that someone else might understand what it means better than she: a healer. Perhaps our stillness in the circle is a response that shows that we begin to grasp the story that is inscribed on her soul.

Intimacy, like healing circles, is another human configuration demanding a sensitivity to details. It is a dense and often confusing setting for communication across specificity. It is a good locus, then, for investigations into the grammar of identity.

LOVERS

Part of what it means to overcome obstacles in the way of our understanding of the world is to insist that we are not defined by contingencies, by what is superficially visible. We insist on the fact that we are individuals who must make individual and highly personal choices. In our attempts to transcend what is purely contingent, we create who we are despite who we seem to be. We create who we are by moving forward in the light of our sense of ourself, in the light of the sense that we make, as Richard Rorty puts it, of the "seemingly random constellation of … things [that] set the tone of a life."[28]

However, in attempting to transcend what is purely contingent about us, we are resisting both obstacles in our souls and obstacles in the world. This is part of what it means to insist on being "heard and seen as individuals with a choice rather than as men marked by what is all too superficially visible," on being free to *determine* as well as to discover our fundamental identity. Some decisions are so fundamentally tied to people's identity that they should not be forced to make them.[29]

There are occasions when commitment to one type of collectivity precludes or is destructive to one's participation in another community, engagement in one type of practice destructive to elements of another sense of the self. One feels compelled to choose between competing and incommensurable values. This may be the case when a woman is drawn to a man who is a stranger to her culture, who indeed might embody harmful representations of her culture. She appears to be confronted by a choice between who she is and who she loves.

It certainly feels as though whom we fall in love with is not something that should be dictated by the collective. It feels like a deeply personal choice: even if our community forces us to marry someone, they cannot force us to love him or her, for that facility is something that is most privately and intimately within us. Just as a collectivity cannot so much as add two and two, so the collectivity cannot fall in love.

The love of idiosyncratic particulars is a hallmark of erotic love. What we love is a smell, an inflection of voice, a way of laughing, the way a particular curve meets a particular angle. What we love is what is in the blood: a singular molecular configuration of DNA, a singular personality with a singular history, a singular birth, a singular identity, a singular destiny.

Aristophanes' description of erotic love in Plato's *Symposium* captures the irresistible sensation that the other half of our identity exists out there, in the world. Aristophanes told the tale of a species of creatures once perfectly spherical and so perfectly content that in their arrogance they scaled the heights of heaven and set upon the gods. To put an end to this disturbance, Zeus cut them in half and dispersed them into the world. He left them with "[a] jagged form, equipped with these oddly lumpy and pointy facial features, these ridiculously exposed and dangling genital members ... like the shape of something that is the object of a joke, or a punishment."[30] Each half was left like the various parts of a jigsaw puzzle with only the combination of specific configurations creating a whole; each was left wandering about with a desperate yearning for the other, questing and clasping at random in search of the other half that would make them both whole.

While humans aspire to be lovers of the Truth – a transcendence of particulars – these creatures are driven by their hunger for the particular. As Martha Nussbaum has noted, "From the inside the disharmony in the nature of these creatures, whose reason still aspires to completeness and control, but whose bodies are so painfully needy, so distracting – from the inside this would feel like torment. From the outside, we cannot help laughing. They want to be gods – and here they are, running around anxiously trying to thrust a piece of themselves inside a hole; or, perhaps more comical still, waiting in the hope that some hole of theirs will have something thrust into it."[31] These creatures delight us.

The allure of erotic love goes beyond its physicality. The sense of an almost fated recognition of another human being extends to a grasp of the disparate elements of his or her character and history. Hephaestus' proposal to weld together Aristophanes' lovers is resonant with an intimation about the capacity of love to heal emotional and moral wounds as well.

This restorative hope for erotic love is movingly captured by one of the resolutions of Morrison's novel, *Beloved*. Sethe's childhood friend – the ex-slave who, when he found out she had murdered her child, stabbed her with his remark "You got two feet, Sethe, not four" – this man came back in the end. "Is it all right, Sethe, if I heat up some water?" he asks.

"And count my feet?" she asks him.

He steps closer. "Rub your feet."

And then:

"Paul D?"

"What, baby?"

"She left me."

"Aw, girl. Don't cry."

"She was my best thing."

Paul D sits down in the rocking chair and examines the quilt patched in carnival colors. His hands are limp between his knees. There are too many things to feel about this woman. His head hurts. Suddenly he remembers Sixo trying to describe what he felt about the Thirty-Mile Woman. "She is a friend of mind. She gather me, man. The pieces I am, she gather them and give them back to me in all the right order. It's good, you know, when you got a woman who is a friend of your mind."

… He leans over and takes her hand. With the other he touches her face. "You your best thing, Sethe. You are." His holding fingers are holding hers.

"Me? Me?"[32]

We are moved and delighted by the restorative possibilities of intimacy. We are aware that we are Aristophanes' creatures. Though we laugh, we suspect that there also may be something tantalizingly impossible, something devastatingly fragile about this love of the particular, as though it merely *appears* possible to behold the contingent other beyond our self-seeking attempts to reach out for ourselves. Not a few of us wait in lonely hope for the one who will gather our pieces and give them back to us in all the right order. In the act of lovemaking, we might momentarily ask, "Is this me? Is everything that I am in this? Does that person moving around inside my body really know anything about *me*?"[33] We might be overcome with the suspicion that the other is asking similar questions.

It is almost as though we must come to the same realization about the other as we do about ourselves. We discover our true love in the same way that we discover ourselves, as if the veracity of the love is a feature of the world. And in the same way that we may be mistaken about the proper characterization of our behaviour, we may be deluded in love.

Not that these tales of disillusion ever truly extinguish the desire to reach out beyond our boundaries. Our very intimate desire for an individual human being is like the desire that bewitches our bodies. It courses through our blood, causing us to be so painfully needy and distracted. This can have a tragic poignancy when erotic love seeks to cross the abyss of culture and blood.

The tantalizing paradox of love across a cultural abyss is that, although it is the particulars of the blood that draws us, the blood carries inherent memories of the collective, and it is this collective memory that constitutes the particular stigma which makes the individual who he or she is. These inherent memories encode not only who we are but also how we act and how we love. If the inherent memory of the collective is one of having been abused, until we heal this memory, we are almost bound to subjugate ourselves. If the inherent memory of the collective is that of the subjugator, we are almost bound to an inescapable sense of entitlement.

Native women, in formulating ways to heal the violence that is going on in their communities, are certainly aware of the power of collective memory:

The colonizer's revisions of our lives, values, and histories have devastated us at the most critical level of all – that of our own minds, our own sense of who we are ...

The portrayal of the squaw is one of the most degraded, most despised and most dehumanized anywhere in the world. The "squaw" is the female counterpart to the Indian male "savage" and as such she has no human face; she is lustful, immoral, unfeeling and dirty. Such grotesque dehumanization has rendered all Native women and girls vulnerable to gross physical, psychological and sexual violence ...

American Indian men [have been depicted] as bloodthirsty savages devoted to treating women cruelly. While traditional Indian men seldom did any such thing ... the lie about "usual" male Indian behavior seems to have taken root and now bears its brutal and bitter fruit.[34]

Just as Indian men and women have difficulty escaping these memories between themselves, so do Native and non-Native couples have difficulty recollecting and burying these memories about each other. It is almost as though history *imposes* a choice on them between who they are and who they love. It is almost inevitable that the more historically powerful continue to subjugate the ones who have always acquiesced. The tortured continue to enrage the torturers by being a living testimony to what they have done. Enraged, the torturers continue. They absorb a history that is not of their individual making. The configuration becomes unseemly, awkward, ugly, brutal.

Louise Erdrich creates such a tragic couple in *Love Medicine*.[35] King is a Chippewa Indian. Lynette, the mother of his child, is described by the King's grandmother as "that white girl." This reduction of Lynette by King's people is reproduced in his words and in his attitude towards her: "'You hear?' King ... barked at Lynette. 'She was calling you. My father's mother. She just told you to do something.'" The reduction of Lynette to a "girl" is reproduced in his words and in his actions. The narrator of the story recollects that she had

adored King's mother into telling me everything she needed to tell ... and it was true, I hadn't understood the words at the time. But she hadn't counted on my memory. Those words stayed with me.

And even now, King was saying something to Lynette that had such an odd dreaming ring to it I almost heard it spoken out in June's voice.

June had said, "He used the flat of his hand. He hit me good." And now I heard her son say "... flat of my hand ... but good ..."

The narrator awakes one night to hear King, in a drunken rage, trying to drown Lynette by pushing her face into a sink of cold dishwater. He only stops drowning the mother of his child when the narrator has jumped on his back and bitten his ear until her mouth fills with blood.

Lynette herself has absorbed a history that obscures her ability to resist the blows. She is too forgiving, too desperate for reconciliation, too quick to forget that he has almost obliterated her. After pulling King off Lynette, the narrator is left alone as the couple departs:

Lynette had turned the lights out in the kitchen as she left the house, and now I heard her outside the window, begging King to take her away in the car.

"Let's go off before they all get back," she said. "It's them. You always get so crazy when you're home. We'll get the baby. We'll go off. We'll go back to the Cities, go home."

And then she cried out once, but clearly it was a cry like pleasure. I thought I heard their bodies creak together, or perhaps it was just the wood steps beneath them, the old worn boards bearing their weight.

They got into the car soon after that. Doors slammed. But they traveled just a few yards and then stopped. The horn blared softly. I suppose they knocked against it in passion. The heater roared on from time to time. It was a cold, spare dawn.

What will their child remember? How will he make sense of this?

If it is true that we have inherent memories of centuries of abuse, then King is not only reacting to the immediate memory of his father beating his mother: he is driven by the inherent memory of being a man in a world that has acquiesced to and normalized male violence. His behaviour is scripted by what generations of men have gotten away with.

But if the underground river of collective memory has run for centuries, then part of King's behaviour is coloured by the fact that he is an Indian and Lynette is white. He is rectifying a manhood tinged with the memory of being an Indian and the memory of years of abuse that Native people have suffered at the hands of European colonizers. Witness the treatment of Indians by Spanish conquistadors of the sixteenth century:

Each of them [the foremen] had made it a practice to sleep with the Indian women who were in his work-force, if they pleased him, whether they were married women or maidens. While the foreman remained in the hut or the cabin with the Indian woman, he sent the husband to dig gold out of the mines; and in the evening, when the wretch returned not only was he beaten or whipped because he had not brought up enough gold, but further, most often, he was bound hand and foot and flung under the bed like a dog, before the foreman lay down, directly over him, with his wife.[36]

The humiliation of Native men has been deep and penetrating.

Is it extraordinary to think that Lynette bears the memory of what her people have done to his? She bears it in her acquiescence, as it is characteristic of women to absorb too much of other people's history while it is characteristic of men to absorb too little. Just as it is characteristic of women to accept that our children take on their father's names and not our own, it is characteristic of women to believe that we can mitigate and heal centuries of violence by embracing where it comes from in our lifetime, tending to the pain of the man in our arms and ignoring the bruises he has left on our bodies and our souls. This capacity of women to absorb too much of other people's history made the marriage of European women to Native men less threatening to the survival of Native culture than the marriage of Native women to European men.

If it is so that Lynette bears the memory of what her people have done to King's, this is also because she bears what centuries of men have done to women. In her acquiescence she bears the memory of degradation and violence that has been done to every woman who has suffered at the hands of men. She bears the memory of every woman in every culture who has been told that her position is as supplicant to man, on her knees, yielding, acquiescing, absorbing blows, spreading her legs. She bears the memory of every woman whose rape is seen as the most potent way to emasculate the manhood of another nation and not as a profound and devastating violation of her own person, her own body, in her own right, not only as a member of a nation but as a woman *and as a human being.*

Both Lynette and King will need to transcend these histories in order to heal as individuals. They will need to transcend these histories in order to be able to love each other and not only be reaching for themselves when they reach for the other. They will need to transcend their own histories before they will be able to build a bridge of love over the troubled river of blood.

HEALING CIRCLES

When you talk about your hurt [in a healing circle], no one makes a
comment, nobody says anything. When we speak it is like holding up a
mirror and asking: what is wrong with me? because nobody else answers.
When you do that you realize the situation you were in. It is no longer
inside of you.   Eva Lepage, community healer, Nunavik 1992

Just as the legal system that sentenced Sethe to jail dealt with the same event as her lover and childhood friend, Paul D, the circuit court in Nunavik often contends with the same desperate acts as healing circles. The gaze that each directs upon these tales is different, at times diametrically opposed. The court focuses on the kind of justice associated with law, healing circles on the kind of justice associated with love, a "realism of compassion." Crudely put, for the court, healing is presumed to come from justice, for the healing circle, justice comes from healing.

To the extent that the court is a transient institution, it frequently lacks common local knowledge. To this extent it remains relatively insensitive to a local sense of justice, indeed even the sense of injustice left behind in its diesel fumes. The community is better equipped than the itinerant plane-load of Qallunaat to perceive the artificiality of the court's sense of propriety. Hence the fact that the fourteen-year-old girl would almost daily have to confront the man at whom she had pointed her finger is nowhere accommodated in the court's methodology, nor is the fact that the parties to the dispute about the van, in a community of 1,400, are likely to have come to a settlement long before the court arrives. Even in the most horrific of cases, the court is precluded from having the kind of complex and multifaceted understanding of the parties that intimacy forces on people.

In small Inuit communities, this kind of intimate knowledge is virtually inescapable. Native police officers have to maintain a near-impossible anomic distance from their community to function. The likelihood is great that an Inuk police officer is related to someone charged with assault. For Inuit social workers to approach a professional goal of dispassionate objectivity would require a contorted amnesia about the web of relations in which they are entangled and in which their lives make sense. The impact of a suicide or homicide will have wrenching personal significance for the whole community.

This intimacy with community pain is familiar enough that the formal bureaucratic gaze of the court is unsettlingly strange and unfamiliar. For the Inuit, the court is dealing not with strangers but with family and community members. The court is not responsive to the way that desperate acts are felt in the community. To this extent, the court is not responsive to the community. The knowledge of intimacy may indeed generate an understanding of the events adverse to the court's findings. However the court construes its actions in these cases, it lacks local authority to ground its legitimacy to the extent of the discrepancy. All it has is force.

Healing circles have the potential to be revelatory of the human being in ways that the court's insight cannot. They are uniquely positioned to recognize what is most fundamentally human behind the superficial descriptions of acts and events. Healing circles deal with the types of suffering that harm people as human beings. They enable individuals to locate themselves in the world, guarding against reactions to the world mediated by those aspects of culture and personality that are "suspect as the marks of submission and fatalism, delusion and escape." Healing circles also focus the participants' attention on the humanity of the other participants. In these ways they foster and preserve the ability of human beings to feel at home in the world.

Healing circles may be more responsive to the way that anguish reverberates through the individual and the community. To this extent they may be generating a parallel, and at times more compelling, sense of justice than the legal justice system. If an obstacle in the soul of an offender and a victim has been removed in the healing circle, then the injustice may have been healed and the need for state legal intervention dissipated. The court may be redundant or counter-productive in these cases.

Healing circles are difficult to describe. This is so not only because of the unique configuration of each circle – a feature that also makes it difficult to generalize about the court in Nunavik – nor only because of the constraint of confidentiality. It is difficult to capture the experiential nature of healing circles and the way in which each participant is implicated. Unlike court, there is no audience in a healing circle. Everybody is a participant. The humanity of each participant is laid bare. How might this be captured in an ethnographic account?

The two tales that set up this chapter would not convey what is transmitted in healing circles. Unlike court where statements are read and testified to in a matter-of-fact tone, people in healing circles are asked to turn their attention to what has hurt them. They are not to recount what had hurt them as if it were a story that had happened to someone else. They are to try and remember the smells, tastes, sights, sounds, and sensations of the event. Similarly, an ethnographer is primarily a participant in the circle and must also revisit her grief. Ethnographic authority would have to come from the ethnographer having been moved not only *by* the intensity of grief released in the circle but moved *from* the situations he was in to its recognition. How might this be measured and conveyed to draw the reader figuratively into the circle?

There is another dimension to healing circles that renders them unsuitable for ethnographic accounts. The ethnographer aspires to penetrate, and be penetrated by, another society. The tacit assumption of ethnography is that there is a boundary between the natural order of the other and that of the self. Unlike the traditional court, which tries individuals and not collectivities, healing circles focus not only on individual violation but on cultural violation. Recognizing the situation one is in also involves seeing the collective dimension to local grief. This liberates the individual who is inhabited by the collective memory.

This focus on the tragic contingencies of birth might seem to be ideally suited to an enterprise emphasizing the diversity and not the universality of human experience. In fact it radically precludes such emphasis. The just and loving gaze of the healing circle also liberates the observers from the obstacles in their soul and allows them to recognize that all participants are "equal members of a natural order which can at any time bring about … a violation of whoever it may be." The order of attention demanded by the healing circle allows its participants to recognize, as Simone Weil describes the revelation, that "I may lose at any moment, through the play of circumstances over which I have no control, anything whatsoever that I possess, including things that are so intimately mine that I consider them as myself."[37] This recognition of an awesome and shared natural order dissolves the fixity of the border from which the ethnographer reports home.

The nature of healing circles and circuit courts suggests that each receives distinct ethnographic treatment. The court is more easily described in the kind of glaring, factual detail that shows up the awkward and bumbling way in which justice is often delivered on the ground. The more abstract rendition of healing circles seems to argue for the kind of justice that comes from healing. There may, however, be an injustice in the different ways that each is represented. The intuitive appeal of healing circles stemming from the benevolent mercy of intimacy may be undermined by a recognition of their inability to reach beyond the circle and alter a fundamentally unjust world just outside their perimeters. This skewed representation of the court and healing circles is highlighted by the ways that healing circles leave intact an imbalance in the ways that men and women relate to each other.

The healing circle's challenge to absorb other people's history places less emotional demands on women than it does on men. Women are trained early to attend to and absorb the needs of others, often at the expense of their own. And for women, forgivingness has a dangerous proximity to acquiescence. The honed and vociferous anger of women, insisting that healing also come from justice, may do more to build a bridge over the abyss of gender than a renewal of tenderness. Healing circles may indeed be unseemly, awkward, and brutal if their beneficent tolerance leaves intact outside their boundaries that part of the natural order in which women and children do not make a comment, do not say anything, and do not answer back.

The court, in this instance, may be better positioned to avoid some of the corruptions of intimacy resulting from too-close contact between human beings. Lynette's too-easy reconciliation with King in *Love*

Medicine would be an illustration of such a corruption of intimacy; perhaps a general rule from the outside of their circle of intimacy would be preferable, one such as "If he raises his hand to you, leave him. Period. Because you are your best thing." This response would not be based exclusively on Lynette's character and personal history but on a more general understanding of the vulnerabilities of women. This corruption of local sense, of the taken-for-granted, can also be seen in the disinclination, conditioned by privilege, to understand oneself from the standpoint of the other's affliction. Some of a community's common sense can stabilize vicious misperceptions of human beings – such as the banality of violence against women – out of the local maldistribution of power. Rectifying inequities in Nunavik may require a more delicate balancing of justice and healing.

In the final tenderness that Paul shows for Sethe in *Beloved*, his personal knowledge of her particular history seems strikingly more revelatory of the human being than the cold and ugly response of the white legal system – the uncontrollable force that both created the Fugitive Bill and sentenced Sethe to jail for murder. The chasm between what Paul and the legal system perceive seems to justify the ascription "white" to the law and hardens the sense that it belongs to one side.

But perhaps there are ways of recounting events that would compel us to feel that sending someone to jail, or otherwise bringing the force of law to bear, is the proper response to a particular act, something a wise judge would do. Is the court always perpetuating cultural oppression when it sentences an Inuk person to a jail term? Could we imagine a wise judge coming to this decision and a shallow judge or ill-equipped community coming to the other? Once again I turn to the allusive nature of the narrative account to explore these questions.

A year after conducting research on family violence in Nunavik I returned to the North for a second stint of fieldwork to witness Nunavik's first sentencing circle. The first period of research in 1992 generated the first narrative account ("Circuit Court/Circus Court") as well as the report that contained the two stories beginning this chapter ("The Children under the Bed"). That report from the summer of 1992, *Family Violence in Kuujjuaq: Talking to Each Other,* found its way into the hands of circuit court judges. It was cited by Judge Dutil in his subsequent written reasons for judgment for the sentencing circle.

This dialogue with the court here comes full circle. The following account is culled from my fieldnotes to the sentencing circle. As with the first account of the court, it serves as a catalyst for rumination.

Circuit/Circus/Circle

COMMUNITY C, NUNAVIK, MAY 1993*

Flying to Community C from Kuujjuaq, we are above the tree line. On the plane are five Qallunaat, including me, who are flying to observe the first sentencing circle in Nunavik. None of us work with the court. Mary Crnkovich, observing for Pauktuutit, had heard of the event in Ottawa and wants to see if the process protects Inuit women's interests. Two lawyers from the Makivik head office are attending the sentencing circle, and a filmmaker from Montréal has been commissioned by the court to film it. We are a diverse group coming up from the South of Canada, having heard about the first Nunavik sentencing circle happening hundreds and hundreds of miles away in a remote geographic area.

The plane drops precipitously. From the window there is still nothing as far as the eye sees but rock and snow and cold grey clouds. But now the rock is steeply banked: these are the highest mountains in Nunavik. As the plane plunges to the earth, I can see the roofs of houses just over the edge of the high rock summit on which the airstrip lies. The municipality covers a geographic area roughly half the size of the McGill University campus.

---

* Mary Crnkovich, in the audience at that sentencing circle observing for Pauktuutit, Canada's Inuit women's association, wrote about what she saw in an article entitled "Report on a Sentencing Circle in Nunavik," *Inuit Women and Justice: Progress Report # 1* (Ottawa: Pauktuutit, 1994). I follow her convention of not identifying the community or participants in the sentencing circle. The community is referred to in that document, as it is here, as Community C.

As we get out of the plane, the air is cold. There is snow on the ground, but it is melting and muddy. The airstrip is the only patch of asphalt in the community. The rest of the roads are made with sand and gravel and have deteriorated in the spring thaw.

Kitty,* the twenty-one-year-old Inuk woman who will house me, picks me up at the airport and drives me to her home. I ask her what she has heard about the sentencing circle which is to happen the next day. She has not heard a thing. I am surprised. Louisa Whiteley knew most of the gossip about her home community, Kuujjuaq, with a population of 1,400, and Community C has one-third as many people. Does Kitty generally know the gossip about Community C? Sure, she says. If she does not know about the sentencing circle, then who, locally, does?

Kitty also tells me she is shy about going to court. She feels that what happens in court is private and that she has no right to be there, listening to other people's business. She would go, however, if someone went with her. She quickly accepts when I invite her.

An hour later, after she has fed me and returned to work, I go for a walk. I can see children looking at me from the windows. From one house, children call out hello.

The sentencing circle is scheduled for the next day. I wake up and, after breakfast, walk over to the co-op hotel where the rest of the group who flew up have stayed. Mary Crnkovich, the filmmaker, and I try to figure out where court will be held. There is no courthouse in Community C. One of us has heard it will take place at the school, so we stroll over and wander through the halls, looking for the court personnel. Classes are in session. We can't find the court anywhere. The principal intercepts us in the hall and introduces himself. He tells us that the court has not yet arrived. He is not sure he can free up any classrooms for it. He brings us down to wait in the nursing office where a dental hygienist is examining students' teeth.

At the end of the morning, the court arrives. The principal gives them a room on the second floor – a laboratory. At the back of the room are glassed-in shelves with microscopes. At the front of the room is a laboratory bench with a sink and gas outlets. On the wall is a map of Northern Canada. Mary notices that Yellowknife is not on it. A poster on the facing wall has an illustration of a seven-car garage and expensive cars

---

* I have changed the names of all of the participants except Judge Dutil, Mary Crnkovich, and Zebedee Nungak, chair of the Inuit Task Force on Justice.

parked along a palm-lined driveway. The poster reads: "The Rewards of Higher Education." The classroom faces one of the strikingly steep mountainsides. Between the mountain and the classroom is a flat, treeless, snow-covered expanse where several huskies are tied.

The judge arrives in his judge's robes. He and the court administrator talk about how to arrange the furniture for the sentencing circle. The judge wants to move the school tables into the middle of the room so they form a square with chairs around them. The court administrator thinks it would be better if there were no tables in the middle, just chairs arranged in a circle.

It becomes clear that there is great deal of confusion about the sentencing circle. The lawyers from Makivik tell us that the mayor thought that the judge was going to gather people for the hearing. The judge had ordered the sentencing circle following the accused's trial in March. The judge thought that Makivik or the mayor were doing the organizing. Makivik thought the probation officer was going to pull the event together. Two hours before it is to begin, no one from the community has been informed or called to the sentencing.

The sentencing circle is not the only case on the docket. The court begins its regular hearings. At the opening of the session, the judge explains that there will be a sentencing circle starting at 2 P.M. He remarks that the case involves a problem that touches many people in Nunavik: family violence. The case will be about this problem as much as about the accused. He wants to know how family violence can be prevented in the communities of Nunavik. He will not necessarily follow the recommendations of the community. There will be no tables. Everyone will sit around in a circle and talk. The judge has the permission of the accused's attorney for the sentencing circle.

He remarks that the circle will be filmed to provide a record which may be useful in the future. The film will not necessarily be distributed to the public and the permission of all those who are present in the circle will be solicited before the film is publicly released. He notes that the accused almost requested the filming. The accused claimed he was not liked in his community. The film was one way for him to get reintegrated. He wanted to share his story with others.

The judge then begins to dispense with the rest of the docket.

There is a break between the regular court session and the sentencing circle. Waiting, people mill about the corridor outside the laboratory, sitting between the winter coats piled up on the children's benches lining the halls.

The victim in the sentencing circle looks to be in her forties, heavy-set. She sits on one of the benches outside the classroom. The accused, her husband, a former police officer, is lean. He too looks to be in his forties. He paces through the corridors. He smiles at me and says hello as he passes.

In the halls waiting for the sentencing circle, Mary Crnkovich and Gail, a Qallunak social worker from Kuujjuaq, talk to the victim, Annie. Gail later tells me that she had spoken to the victim on the phone about the sentencing circle and described to her what was going to happen. But when Mary and Gail sit down with her now, Annie says she was unaware that it was going to take place. Gail tells her again about the circle. She also tells her that she will have to say what had happened and how she felt. Mary informs her that the sentencing will be filmed. This is news to Annie. No one has asked her permission. Her husband calls her away as she is talking to Mary and Gail.

The accused, Willie, has been living in Community B for the last three months since his conviction, as per court order. He was to stay away from his wife pending sentencing. However, he arrived in Community C a day before the court and has been speaking to his wife during the last twenty-four-hour period.

As we wait, Gail informs me she had to argue with the provincial police on Annie's behalf to get them to go to Community C to charge Willie. At that point Annie had fled from his attacks to Kuujjuaq to stay in Nunavik's only battered woman's shelter. There used to be an Inuk police officer in Community C but she stopped working in March 1993. By the time of the sentencing circle, Community C still lacks a police officer. The Inuit police officers are given guns but are not trained how to use them if there is an incident involving a firearm. If there is a problem that requires police assistance, people are to go to the mayor, who will act as a constable. He, too, is not trained to deal with firearm incidents. If the mayor cannot solve the problem, the Sureté du Québec in Kuujjuaq must be contacted. It takes at least two hours for the provincial police to fly from Kuujjuaq to Community C.

Gail tells me that the police who gave her trouble about flying up to charge Willie complained to her when they came back about having been sent. A brother-in-law of the accused had given the police trouble. The police thought that Annie was lying. They eventually charged Willie, who was sent to detention in the South so Annie could return to her home.

I find out from the probation officer that the accused was previously charged and convicted of sexually assaulting a woman in the back seat of the police car while he was a police officer. He was in uniform when the incident occurred. He was convicted approximately six years ago.

NUNAVIK'S FIRST SENTENCING CIRCLE

Just after 2 P.M., the court is ready for the sentencing circle. We file in. A middle-aged Inuk woman asks me if it is all right to go in. I tell her it is okay, that the court is a public place.

In the centre of the room the chairs are arranged in a circle. At the back of the classroom are two rows of chairs for those who are witnessing the circle but not participating. In the recess the judge invited Mary Crnkovich to sit in the circle and contribute. She declined, saying that she did not come from the community.

Kitty has turned up to witness the sentencing circle. As she is entering the room with me, Mary tells her that she can go and sit in the circle of chairs, which she does, likely unaware that I will not be following her to the circle and that she has thereby been made a participant.

Sitting in the circle are the Crown prosecutor, the mayor of Community C, an Inuk community health worker, Gail (the social worker from Kuujjuaq), the probation officer, defence counsel, the accused, the victim, the court translator, the judge, Jessie (sister of victim), Adamie (victim's elderly brother-in-law), Penena (mother of accused), Mallee (sister of accused), Kitty, and Kathie (Willie's sister-in-law, cousin of Annie). The couple sit next to each other.

In the audience at the start of the sentencing there are three Inuit people. This number grows and shrinks over the session as people enter to observe for a period and then leave and are replaced by others. The Inuit observers sit on chairs or on the floor, or they stand, leaning on the laboratory bench at the end of the classroom. Among the Qallunaat people sitting in the audience are Mary Crnkovich, myself, some of the defence lawyers, the two Qallunaat lawyers from Makivik, and the court clerk. There is not much room. Coats and boots are piled on the floor and over chairs. At the other side of the classroom, the filmmaker prepares to film the sentencing.

The group sits quietly in the circle for about ten minutes. They are waiting for Zebedee Nungak to turn up. He is flying from Community A to attend the circle. When he has not appeared at the end of this period, the judge starts the session at 2:30 P.M. He has taken off his judge's cape for the sentencing circle. He launches right in:

JUDGE: Three months ago, Willie pleaded guilty to charges of assault on his wife as well as to breach of probation for the same offence. The probation order specified that he was not to harass his wife.

Willie said he was not happy at his trial because ten years ago, he had had an experience with the court that had harmed him. He also felt he was not accepted in the community. He admitted to having beaten his wife between fifty and one hundred times. He is asking for help from his people.

The judge stops talking while this is translated. Zebedee Nungak arrives at this point and takes a seat. Once he is settled, the session proceeds. The court translator works from Inuktitut to English and back throughout the session until later on Zebedee Nungak takes the translation upon himself.

JUDGE: Sentencing circles have been tried in Saskatchewan and the effects of them appears to be that criminality goes down as the accused are sentenced by their own people, not by a judge. The recent Inuit Task Force on Justice also talks about something similar. It recommends that [he reads from the report] the present court system should provide for community participation and involvement in the sentencing process.

I want to stress that I am on the same level as everyone who is here in the circle for this sentencing. I am not a judge. We are all together, the same. The question we have to answer here today is: What are we going to do?

PENENA (mother of accused): Can we answer that question?

JUDGE: Yes.

PENENA: Even if they send people down south, they are still with white people who have different languages. Even when they come back from down there there is no improvement. It is better if people with the same language and lifestyle try to help.

I am happy the court is starting to do something. There are a lot of people who know how to help but then the accused go to court and are sentenced. They cannot go further as the Inuit cannot get involved.

ZEBEDEE NUNGAK: I want to explain the presence of the camera here. This video is being made as this is the first time the circle is being tried in the region. The video is not to be shown to anyone without the participants' consent.

Perhaps the judge covered this ground, but as chair of the Task force, when I was invited to attend, I accepted because the people of Nunavik have wanted to be more involved in how people in the justice system are treated. Today is not normal because usually the person broke a law and that is the only thing on the court's mind. After all the decisions are made, then the sentence is given.

Now it is up to the circle to determine what is the best thing to do about Willie to help him to get a fresh start. This is an opportunity not just for him but for others that may be treated in a healing circle like this.*

MALLEE (sister of accused): In the past, the accused was sent to jail. Two times I went to see my brother in jail in Waterloo. We didn't have long to talk. He asked how everyone was at home. There was no time to talk about his life.

When Willie was in Community B, I went to see him. We had time to talk as it was an Inuit place and he didn't miss too much about home. He talked of his life. We were trying to find a solution.

It is better to let the accused stay in an Inuit village. It is better for their life. In Community B, we were talking of our feelings. We talked of our family because the place is different.

MAYOR: All people have different lifestyles. The last time Willie was sentenced he was thinking about what he should do, and I am thankful for that. We know Willie and want to help him. Willie said he did not feel welcome anymore. We always welcome people even if they do something bad. Feeling unwanted is in the mind. We need to find a solution.

ADAMIE (victim's elderly brother-in-law): In the beginning the judge asked what to do with Willie and how we can help him. I know the couple. The wife is the sister of my wife. I know she is tired of being treated badly. I met the husband on the plane. I felt sorry for him even if he committed an offence. I think women are weaker than men and don't deserve to be beaten. Couples should talk. Since I have been growing up, I have learned good and bad. I still learn what is good and bad. If Willie is trying to improve himself, he should be helped right away.

---

* The judge, throughout the session, also refers to the sentencing circle alternatively as a healing circle and a sentencing circle. The two are different phenomena.

JUDGE: How?

KATHIE (Willie's sister-in-law, cousin of Annie): The first thing to do is to be open to him so he can talk to us when he has problems. We need to pray together. There should be more communication.

JESSIE (sister of victim): I am glad I was invited. In the past in my family, especially with my two younger sisters, there were family members sent to jail. Even when my sister's husband was sent to jail, I never thought I was glad he was in jail because he was brought to jail and no one but the court had had a chance to talk. It is good now that the community can talk. It is best that Willie talk and tell us what he needs. Jail is not a solution. Sometimes we say we want things to get better but nothing happens. This is the best way to find a solution. I feel Willie should open up and let others get a sense of where he stands.

WILLIE: I want to give a description of how I have lived my life. The abuse on my wife has been physical and also verbal, for example by what I say to her. In my experience, my wife has gone through both abuses. When I was arrested the first time, I had it in my mind that my behaviour would improve as a result of going to jail. The second time I was arrested for the same thing, I was sentenced to a longer term in jail. I thought that would cure my problem. But still there was no cure for the fact that I was an abuser. For the third arrest, I had to think. I wondered whether I would continue on this cycle of abuse and jail. I wondered what I could do to alter my behaviour. I never wanted to be an abuser. I do not admire people who batter. I do not want to be one who causes conflict among my people.

Long after I was abusing my wife, I tried to keep it a secret from the community as I thought I could fix the problem myself. I didn't want a reputation as an abuser so I tried to keep it secret, hoping I could find a cure in the meantime. But eventually, my wife suggested that I needed help for my behaviour. I did not want help because I thought I had the inner strength.

JUDGE: Are your people willing to give you help?

JESSIE: Yes, we are willing and able to provide help to Willie. It is easy to provide help because for the first time we are given an opportunity to speak up and help and for the first time, it is revealed to us that Willie is open to receiving help. We did not know this before. So for those reasons, it is possible for the community to extend help to Willie as he now says he needs help and will take it.

WILLIE: The big problem is that once I seem to resolve the problem I am having, for example if the problem is jealousy and I try to deal with that and find a cure for that, other causes appear that I have not thought of before. I am ashamed to be the cause of attention because I am behaving this way. Something else always comes up. I wonder: will I go on running after something I cannot catch? I sympathize with my family as I am putting them through these problems. I wonder what is wrong with me.

After reflecting on what I have said, I feel there is a solution. I want to allow others to speak first before saying what that solution is.

MALLEE: Willie used to have many good qualities. He has had responsible jobs before his problems overcame him. He was a teacher, police officer, was working at the airport, director for the school. He was competent ... so many good things. It seems that the positive experiences were dropped as his problems overcame him. Certain things were no longer open to him – for example, he could no longer be a police officer as you cannot assault someone and then be a police officer. He dropped these positive experiences after his arrests. He tried to keep secret his behaviour from his parents. Though our parents tried to do their best, he kept things a secret.

Now I feel Willie has to be very open to his parents and to the elders in the community to receive help. If he deals with this alone, the problem is too big. He cannot do it on his own. If the mayor extends help, he should be totally open to that. Willie should commit himself to keep open.

JUDGE: It is now 4 P.M. We'll take a brief recess and meet again in ten minutes.

During the recess, the judge asks Mary Crnkovich how she thinks things are going. He is thinking of winding things up. She feels that things have just started and that there really has not been much of substance that has been said. The judge takes this in and remarks that he wants to hear from the wife.

After about ten minutes, people return to the room and settle into their places. The judge, having been reminded by the filmmaker in the recess, asks people to go around the room and introduce themselves, which they do.

JUDGE: Many people have been talking so far in the healing circle, including Willie. I would be interested in hearing from the victim.

ANNIE: I am thankful for the healing circle. In the past I have been asked how we can get help. I have said he needs help in the past. For now, that is what I am going to say.

JUDGE (to the circle): Will you provide him with help? How? Who?

KATHIE: We can help him among the people if he asks us for help. When we, the Inuit, see others are having trouble, we help. If he opens himself up, we will help.

ADAMIE (to the judge): Will you send him to jail if there is no help here? Everyone here will help if he doesn't lie to us. If he lies to us, I don't mind if he gets sent to jail. If there are only words and no action, things will stay the same. I want to ask the judge something: is there a choice for the community to assure the judge that we will help him if he stays, or might the judge take him away?

JUDGE: I am not ready to answer that question yet. Right now, Willie lives in Community B. Do you want him to come back to Community C?

KATHIE: I think it is better for Willie to come back to Community C for the cohesion of the family because his wife is struggling to bring up the children and that is a burden to her. If he gives an honest try, then we should have him back.

JUDGE: Does his wife want him back?

ANNIE: Yes. My concern is that there are many children to look after. It is a burden to bring them up properly without a father, so I want him to come back.

MAYOR: If there can be proper supervision of the offender then maybe he could come back. Even if he is on probation, there is no probation officer here in Community C so he must meet regularly with the mayor or a social worker. But when offenders slack off and don't report properly, that supervision tends not to have effect any more. If Willie agrees to meet with me or a social worker on a scheduled basis, if he is honest about starting afresh, I would welcome him back readily. Willie used to be a good influence in the community. Perhaps he can start those good things again. He needs a supervision schedule so he can offer to make a fresh start. I also want to hear Willie's solution so the group can help with that.

PENENA: I would like to see, in the community, men becoming more vocal about the problem of physical abuse so people can figure out how the problem can be eliminated. I want more visibility of Inuit tradition and practices in which the bonds amongst men were strong enough to prevent abuse. Men need to get together to find ways to prevent abuse. Men need to participate to let the community know that abuse is not acceptable.

JUDGE: I wonder if the probation officer has anything to add?

PROBATION OFFICER: I will wait to hear from Willie first.

WILLIE: I had the experience of meeting with a probation officer on a scheduled basis. I feel that this is not adequate as I am the only one getting attention. I want designated contact people, a support group, who can meet with me to discuss my progress and my problems. I have discussed this with my wife and I want people to support me, but I want somewhere where my wife can go also. My wife should be able to seek help from designated people. Some people should be designated for support for me and my wife together to complement help from the probation officer.

(MALLEE asks Zebedee Nungak a question to which he answers)

ZEBEDEE NUNGAK: As an observer, I agree with what Willie's mother mentioned regarding more meetings in the community where the problem of abuse is discussed to scale down the problem. Willie mentioned he would submit to attending a support group. The community should put that together. Responsible people should establish a group. There may be others that can take advantage of that support. There must be others who need help. The community should form a support group like Alcoholics Anonymous. I cannot say this is a great idea as I do not know the community.

GAIL: One of the biggest problems is the secrecy. It is hidden. The community needs to build in some outlets. Last time, the woman was hiding it for a long time. She was scared to talk. The woman does not have any outlets to talk. People need to start opening up to talking about it. With that, change comes.

JESSIE (translated by Nungak): In forming such a support group, much thought should be given to the selection of people. The mayor and social worker can be approached, but some people are still not open to people if they have special problems. If there is a support group, we need to think carefully about the qualities of individuals. The group should include elders strong in traditional culture, who have wisdom to share.

I do not belittle the role of the court and justice people, but it is plain to see there is a role that local people have to play. There is a role for local people in solving these problems. Problems are continuing to multiply so we need help from whatever source. I am thankful for this opportunity. I want in the future to continue this co-operative approach.

ZEBEDEE NUNGAK (makes a statement in Inuktitut, then): I want to ask for clarification regarding whether the court is now dealing with the assault offence or is Willie in Community B for another offence.

JUDGE: He is in Community B as it is one of the conditions for him to be free that he has no contact with his wife. He is not in jail in Community B. But Community B is a better place for him than Community C. The charge is assault.

CROWN PROSECUTOR: Willie has been convicted two prior times for assault on his wife. He was on probation for the same thing when he assaulted his wife again.

(ZEBEDEE NUNGAK says something in Inuktitut. The following exchanges are in Inuktitut with no translation.

WIFE'S SISTER responds.

ZEBEDEE NUNGAK responds to wife.

MAYOR comments.

WIFE'S SISTER responds.

WILLIE comments.

MAYOR responds.)

ZEBEDEE NUNGAK (translating): We were having a discussion on how the members of the community can assure the court that the community will do something tangible. One question is whether it should be done first with consulting Willie and his wife regarding who they can open up to and share with. If the individuals are not trustworthy enough for Willie and his wife to open up to, then it is no good.

The mayor wants a support group for spousal assault. He wants to ask Willie and his wife who they can talk with. If they cannot name someone, he will work with the social worker and council to come up with a list of people. Willie says that people say he has to talk about it. He is willing to take that advice and to talk about his behaviour. No one comes to mind right away, but he will submit to a group. The mayor will get together a support group for Willie and his wife and for others in the community with the same problem.

JUDGE: When will that be formed?

MAYOR (via Zebedee Nungak): We can give it emergency attention and can come up with the names of individuals this week.

JUDGE: What does the crown think?

CROWN PROSECUTOR: We can provide the names of those involved in the same crime so they can benefit as well. The accused said he will submit to that. Perhaps the accused can bring people who are in the same situation. If Willie is willing to have counselling, the Crown is willing to give it a chance.

I also want to know: if something happens from now to the end of the decision of the court, we have to make sure the wife will tell right away and not hide it.

JUDGE: Willie appeared before me in Kuujjuaq. We all agreed that instead of detention, he would wait in Community B where he would have no contact with his wife. The sentence was postponed until today. A group is not formed. So what will I do with him: send him back to Community B, in which case I will not sentence him until October when I come back again? Timing is a problem. When I sent Willie to Community B, I wanted to protect his wife and him. If such a group exists, he and his wife will go to the group and there will be supervision of his behaviour.

I agree that the court does not come often. I am going to adjourn this meeting for now and we will meet again today. The mayor and Willie are to discuss if there is a group they can agree on. If there is such a group, I may render a decision that Willie can come back on bail. He has to report to the group once a week. Then in October I will see how the group is going.

I will want to see that group in October. Tonight I want the names of people that Willie and his wife will report to.

The non-Inuit people leave the room. The Inuit people from the circle remain behind to discuss the question of who will be in the group.

During this break, Mary Crnkovich reminds the judge that the wife has done nothing wrong and cannot be "sentenced" to attend a support group.

5:45 P.M.: The court reconvenes in the circle.

MAYOR: The first preference was to consult with Willie and his wife to have who they trust. Through that process, we named two people. Then others at the circle named a third. Two are suggested by the couple: myself, and Kathie. The third person is Lizzie who is the social assistant for Community C.

JUDGE: Is Kathie related to any of the parties?

MAYOR: Yes. She is Willie's brother's wife.

JUDGE: Is the fact that she is related not a problem?

ZEBEDEE NUNGAK: She is the most trusted of the wife. The wife trusts her.

GAIL: The wife had talked to me earlier. Kathie was the choice of the wife.

ZEBEDEE NUNGAK: They are cousins and grew up together.

JUDGE (to Willie and Annie): Are you happy with the choice?

WILLIE AND ANNIE: Yes.

JUDGE: Now the healing circle is finished.

As part of Willie's conditions, I imposed an undertaking that he live in Community B. He was not to directly or indirectly communicate with his wife.

Now there is a group where Willie and his wife will go. His wife cannot be forced to go; however, it is a good thing if she goes.

As part of the new conditions, Willie can come back now. The condition not to communicate is gone. The condition to keep the peace until the end of the proceeding remains. He also has a prohibition against drinking and he cannot go to a bar.

So the new conditions are that he can come back. He can communicate with his wife as he will live with her. There is a condition not to molest or verbally harass her. He has to report to the group of three people that was formed today. "To report" means to discuss with the group. On October 19, I will be back. I will adjourn the sentence on that date and inquire about how the group and Willie worked. I will ask if he went every week. I also want to see Willie's wife. Are there any other suggestions?

GAIL: If the conditions are not met, what recourse does the wife have? Who is she to report to?

JUDGE: She is to report to the probation officer because he comes here.

PROBATION OFFICER: Willie is already on probation so anyhow I will be involved. If something happens, call me or the police; or the mayor can call me. We'll deal with it.

JUDGE: I want to thank everyone. This was the first healing circle in Québec. I was moved by people and by the volunteers who came out.

POST-SENTENCING IMPRESSIONS

The judge and Zebedee Nungak are interviewed for the film at the end of the sentencing. Neither has a negative comment.

In an interview after the sentencing, the probation officer tells me that there is just an undertaking for Willie to go to the group. He cannot supervise an undertaking, only a sentence. His only official duty is to supervise the probation order not to molest the victim and to keep the peace. The wife has to go to the police otherwise. As there are no police in Community C, she has to call the police in Kuujjuaq. Later, he tells me that his supervisor informed him that he will have to supervise the undertaking even though it is not within his mandate.

Kitty tells me later that night that one of the best things about the sentencing circle is that people get to pick who they want to talk to. They are more likely to go if they can pick who they see. She knows a batterer who could benefit from the support group, as could other couples she knows where violence is a problem.

In an interview later in the week, the judge again remarks that he thinks that the sentencing circle went well. It had been very hard to organize. He had wanted to try the sentencing circle on a family violence case as this problem has reached epidemic proportions in the North. He wanted to see if the community could start to take control of the issue rather than giving it to the Qallunaat justice system.

I ask him if he could play a role in making sure that the circle is not stacked with the accused's family members or that the mayor is not prejudicially involved in the case. He says he relies on the mayor and on the probation officer to make those decisions. For this circle, he only specified that he wanted elders, women, and the mayor. He tells me that the probation officer was responsible for selecting this circle and had done so. Could he imagine coming up to the community for, say, two weeks before the trial to get a sense of the community and to help select the people that would be most suitable for a particular sentencing circle? That would not be appropriate, he says, because it would compromise his neutrality in the case. He again emphasizes that he relied on the probation officer to get that kind of information for him. When I ask him about whether he thought that vulnerable members of the community might be left in a precarious situation with the sentencing circle, he replies that he does not see how.

He also notes that the court is willing to give the justice system to the Inuit but the Inuit need to take it. The Inuit are passively resistent to taking control. He had to struggle to get Zebedee Nungak to attend the sentencing circle.

I later ask the probation officer to comment on the judge's remark that the probation officer was responsible for organizing the circle and that he had done so. He says he had been told to get people together, so he contacted the mayor and passed the task on to him. As far as the probation officer is concerned, organizing a circle is too political for him. Community C is not his community and, furthermore, it is not in his mandate to select a circle. He also remarks that the Crown did not bring up Willie's prior conviction for sexual assault because sentencing circles are too political.

The Crown prosecutor feels that the sentencing circle was not a good idea in a family violence case. He communicated this concern to the judge before sentencing. He would have suggested an upcoming narcotics case in another community. There, the community is more involved as it is a community problem. He also feels that the mayor of that community tends to be neutral in his advice on sentencing, siding with neither friends nor enemies – something he could not say about the mayor of Community C. Ordinarily, he tells me, if this had been a regular trial, Willie would have had a prison term more severe than the last one. The accused has two prior convictions with prison sentences for the same offence. The Crown had remained as silent as he did because he wanted the community to have a chance to be involved. He had been told to just be there. He was given no other role.

POSTSCRIPT

Willie had his final sentencing hearing in the fall of 1993. He was given a three-year term of probation to be served in the community. One of the conditions of probation was that he continue to meet with the local committee set up in the sentencing circle. Six weeks later he was charged with sexual assault against a relative of his wife. He pleaded guilty to the charge and was sentenced in May of 1994 to eighteen months of detention to be served in the Waterloo Correctional Centre. After serving twelve months he was released back to the community in May of 1995. During the summer of 1995 he was again charged with sexual assault. Preliminary hearing for this offence was scheduled for early November 1995.

Agents of Justice/
Agents of Love

A recurring worry in the literature and case law on sentencing in Canadian criminal law is that it fails to ensure that every individual is treated equally before and under the law. Apart from a small list of maximum and minimum sentences, the Criminal Code is silent about specifying determinate sentences for each determinate criminal act. Sentencing is essentially left to "the discretion of the court that convicts a person who commits the offense."[1] Although provincial courts of appeal theoretically review judicial discretion in sentencing, these courts are similarly unconstrained by the explicit codification of principles that provides order to substantive criminal law. While there is a range of defensible approaches to sentencing, there is a fear that, within the range, judges may justify almost any outcome.

The Canadian Sentencing Commission gave voice to this anxiety in its report *Sentencing Reform: A Canadian Approach (1987)* : "it is almost impossible for any sentence handed down in Canada to be judged unambiguously unjust. Given there are an almost infinite (or at least a very large) number of dimensions on which two cases can vary, and given that there are no over-riding principles that specify either a priority system of purposes of sentence or the weight that should be given to different factors, almost any two cases can be differentiated along at least one dimension that could justify differential sentencing."[2] Furthermore, judges must weigh specific facts and circumstances in sentencing. These contextual elements are unique and diverse. This particularization appears to nullify the possibilities for equal treatment across cases.

One school of thought proposes to remedy the over-contextualization of sentencing with more articulated rules approximating the uniformity of codified criminal law.[3] Justice would be rendered by linking sentences with the criminal act, not the criminal; with the abstract text, not the concrete instance. Judges would be confronted with a legal syllogism: if x, then y; if crime x, then sentence y. The rule seems to apply itself. Any judge, in any court, in any case, confronted with any crime, must come to the same conclusion on sentencing. So goes the thinking.

This move would seem to generate hermetically sealed criteria for sameness. However, its logic is only apparently impermeable to idiosyncrasy. As one of the leading Canadian cases on sentencing noted, "Even putting aside the offender's circumstances, those who advocate some form of fixed sentences fail to appreciate that the definitions of the crimes in the *Criminal Code* contain only certain key elements required for guilt. For example, the definition of robbery requires only the taking of the property of another accompanied by an act of violence. The elements for guilt are the same whether the offence involves an elaborate bank holdup or, literally, taking candy from a baby."[4] Similarly, taking a van in Kuujjuaq without the owner's permission is the strict equivalent of auto theft in Montréal.

In order to close up these openings with rules, the Criminal Code would need to be voluminously large, specific, and detailed to ensure that *only* the *same* crimes are treated in the same way. Furthermore, the notion of "same crime" is something that will need to be decided on particular facts. And the determination of whether an act is the same as a textbook definition will require some interpretation on the part of a judge or jury, fitting the text to the peculiar circumstances of the case. And if a rule stands in need of an interpretation, then it cannot apply itself. Now the refined order of the Criminal Code seems on shaky ground.

These concerns about how to render justice when justice requires, in part, paying attention to context and idiosyncratic details are reflected in the sentencing circle and in overall questions about reforming the delivery of legal justice in Nunavik. It sometimes appears that incommensurable sets of values and practices need to be reconciled to a single frame of reference for justice to be done. If the court nowhere attends to the specificities of Inuit culture, it remains insensitive to a local sense of injustice; but attending to the needs of an Inuit community can entail balancing needs that may seem incommensurable – the need for local input into the legal system and the need of women, anywhere, to be protected from violence. It seems like a general rule must be formulated in order to know how to proceed: but how does a general rule incorporate diverse, incommensurable understandings about how to proceed?

Before returning to the moral dilemmas to which Nunavik's first sentencing circle gives rise, I want to take an excursion into legal theory to find a way of thinking about law that is broad enough to suggest accommodations between incommensurable practices and values: to look for a way of thinking about law that does not insist that making diverse legal sensibilities commensurable means measuring them all by the same (usually metropolitan) standard. Because sentencing law falls notoriously short of that presumed standard with its insistently contextual references to "fit," it is a good place to begin examining the peculiar nature of our general expectations about predictability and constraint in law.

THE CONSTRAINT OF LAW

The anxiety about the indeterminacy of rules for sentencing echoes Wittgenstein's preliminary speculations that "an indefinite boundary is not really a boundary at all. Here one thinks perhaps: if I say 'I have locked the man up fast in the room – there is only one door left open' – then I simply haven't locked him in at all; his being locked in is a sham. One would be inclined to say here: 'You haven't done anything at all.' An enclosure with a hole in it is as good as *none*."[5] Critics of Canadian sentencing law are similarly tempted to say that without explicit, nondiscretionary rules covering moves in sentencing, there is virtually no constraint on judges. A rule requiring contextual interpretation is as good as none. Wittgenstein continued his speculation by asking, "But is that true?" Is it true of sentencing?

Wittgenstein's subsequent discussion about rule-following has implications for more than just the principles of sentencing. It throws in relief not just what we are doing when we have someone submit to the criminal justice system but what we are doing when we talk about rule following in law generally. Any rule-governed activity, whether explicit, textual, and institutionalized, or implicit, oral, and informal, appears to fall prey to the rule-sceptical observation that rules do not apply themselves.

An illustration of this quandary comes up in the literature on sentencing Inuit offenders. Condemning a Qallunaat and an Inuit offender convicted under the same criminal code offence to the same jail term in the same institution looks as though it treats both in the same manner. However, features such as language and remoteness from home make jail terms more unbearable for an Inuk. Imprisonment for a northern Native offender would produce "a loneliness that would be greater than that in isolation."[6] Part of what it means to be *tigujaumaju* – to be taken away by an uncontrollable force – is to be taken away to a foreign land by a foreign people. Following the rule about punishing the same offence with the same sentence would mean treating Inuit offenders differently than Qallunaat offenders, taking into account the distinctive peculiarities of their circumstances as Inuit.

Sentencing circles also illustrate the quandary about how we know when different things receive the same treatment. Because his community contributes to the sentencing determination, the offender who goes to jail is not *taken* away but *sent* away. Restoring control to the offender's people means that the offender's remaining sense of *tigujaumaju* is individual. Further protest would appear self-interested and unreasonable to his people. To this extent, the Inuit would be no more foreigners to the criminal justice system than any other Canadian. But, as in Nunavik's first sentencing circle, what if the offender receives a lesser sentence than would his counterpart in the South? A Qallunaat batterer with two prior prison terms for assault would have received a more severe sentence than counselling. Are Inuit women, as victims of assault, treated with the same regard as Qallunaat victims? Are the Inuit people then treated in the same manner by the criminal justice system as other Canadians?

The dilemma in sentencing, and more generally in any rule-governed activity, is the dilemma about what it means to go on in the "same" way, what it means to treat two cases alike, what it means to say there is a fit between the general rule and the particular instance. Superficially one might respond that someone is following a rule if she always acts in the same way in the same circumstances. But this response begs the questions. It assumes that there is an absolute unchanging sense to the words "the same." But we do not know whether two things are to be regarded as the same or not unless we are told the context in which the question arises.

The superficial response to the question about what it means to treat two cases alike amounts to saying that the rule tells you how to go on in the same way, or, legally speaking, that the law tells you how it is to be applied in particular circumstances. This appears to be like saying that a signpost tells you not only which direction to proceed but how to follow the direction of the signpost. But this does not make sense. Wittgenstein set up this formulation of the problem: "A rule stands there like a sign-post. – Does the sign-post leave no doubt open about the way I have to go? Does it shew which direction I am to take when I have passed it; whether along the road or the footpath or cross-country? But where is it said which way I am to follow it; whether in the direction of its finger or (e.g.) in the opposite one? – And if there were, not a single sign-post, but a chain of adjacent ones or of chalk marks on the ground – is there only *one* way of interpreting them?"[7] If going in the opposite direction of the head of the arrow is one way of following the arrow (following it always in the opposite direction), then the rule does not, in and of itself, direct the way it is to be interpreted.

Any number of interpretations can be seen to be following the rule in some sense. Wittgenstein gave the simple mathematical example of asking someone to continue the series 1,2,3,4 ... in the same way. Some-one might go on in the same way by writing down 1,2,3,4,1,2,3,4,5,6,7,8 ... It is not difficult to extrapolate from this that if one provides a suffi-ciently complex rule, any way of going on will be a continuation of the original series.

This is not far from what commonly happens in legal argument. Both parties to a dispute seek out sufficiently complex justifications for inter-preting the law in their favour. By choosing an extremely basic example of a series and showing how a complex interpretation will constitute going on in the same way, Wittgenstein goes some distance to curing us of the easy case/hard case distinction in law. Surely if the mathematical series 1,2,3,4 ... does not contain, in itself, the way to continue, then nothing constitutes, in itself, an easy case.

One is tempted, in the face of the fact that the signpost does not also tell us which way it is to be read, to say that there must be some further direction that tells us how to follow the sign-post: an interpretation, something outside of the rule that tells us how it is to be read. This would stand like a meta-rule to the rule, the spark plug that starts the engine in motion. But this cannot be correct. Wittgenstein points out that interpretations still leave rules indeterminate: "'But how can a rule shew me what I have to do at *this* point? Whatever I do is, on some interpretation, in accord with the rule.' – That is not what we ought to say, but rather: any interpretation still hangs in the air along with what it interprets, and cannot give it any support. Interpretations by them-selves do not determine meaning."[8]

Rules cannot, logically, always stand in need of interpretation as the interpretation itself is a rule. This implies an infinite regress, each inter-pretation having an interpretation behind it to indicate how to interpret the interpretation of the rule, each ungrounded, hanging in the air.[9] In the face of this regress, there must be a way of following a rule that is not an interpretation. At some point interpretations must come to an end in a particular instance of obeying the rule and going against it. "If I have exhausted the justifications I have reached bedrock, and my spade is turned. Then I am inclined to say: 'This is simply what I do.'"[10]

Because neither rules nor interpretations apply themselves, there is a temptation to conclude that rules are meaningless: "Whatever I do is, on some interpretation, in accord with the rule." Because every move is permissible, none is. If a rule stands always in need of interpretation, and an interpretation can read the rule in any way, then in what sense can the rule be said to be pointing in any direction at all?

In law, as in philosophy, one is left with a kind of vertigo where everything seems arbitrary. If anything can, on some interpretation, be in accord with the legal rule, then there is no internal constraint in law. If anything can be in accord with the legal rule, then it becomes hard to say that someone has made a mistake, that a judge has interpreted the law incorrectly, that a particular sentence is inappropriate, unfit, unjust. The idea of law as autonomous, internally coherent, and determined is illusion, if not ideology.

Wittgenstein suggests another way to ground rule-following behaviour which recurs to neither interpretations nor to the rules themselves. "Then can whatever I do be brought into accord with the rule?" asks his interlocutor. He responds:

Let me ask this: what has the expression of a rule – say a sign-post – got to do with my actions? What sort of connexion is there here? – Well, perhaps this one: I have been trained to react to this sign in a particular way, and now I do so react to it.

But that is only to give a causal connexion; to tell how it has come about that we now go by the sign-post; not what this going-by-the-sign really consists in. On the contrary; I have further indicated that a person goes by a sign-post only in so far as there exists a regular use of sign-posts, a custom.[11]

We follow rules in a particular way because we are trained in the use of the rule. The bedrock that is reached when interpretations have come to an end is a custom of following rules. We have learned to use words and objects along with other people grouped around a common activity. Anyone who has learned elementary mathematics will continue the series 1,2,3,4 … by writing down 5,6,7,8, etc. *as a matter of course.* As Peter Winch noted, "the very fact that I have been able to write 'etc.' after those figures and that I can be confident of being taken in one way rather than another by virtually all my readers, is itself a demonstration of the same point."[12] We continue as a matter of course because of commonalities in our training in the regular use of mathematical formulae. The criteria for following a rule correctly come from the practice that has developed around the rule and which the participant has learned. A mistake is a contravention of what has been *established* as correct.

The rule does not direct one in an absolute sense: it is the practice around the rule that determines how it is to be followed and whether it is followed correctly. Rules may sometimes leave room for doubt and sometimes not. This will depend on whether the practice that uses the rules is settled between the practitioners, whether they share agreements in judgment: "And now this is no longer a philosophical question, but an empirical one."[13]

The practice may change and require that the rule be read in a different way. This is the realist point in law – if an arrow is consistently read in the opposite direction of its head, this practice *becomes* the new rule about how the arrow is to be followed. Law is not (only) what is written in texts: law is what officials do about disputes. But sometimes officials, in doing something about the dispute, are following the rules *without* interpretation. And this, to put a fine point on it, is no longer a philosophical question but an *empirical* one.

This analysis does not construe practices as the product of obedience to the rules but rather sees rules as gaining their intelligibility from the practices in which they are imbedded. The constraint of law is not a set of rules but dispositions, inculcated early and constantly reinforced by a community of individuals similarly disposed. Bourdieu calls this configuration of dispositions the "habitus," the "durably installed generative principle of regulated improvisations," the presupposed linguistic and cultural competence that makes communication possible, gives the social world its self-evident, natural character, and causes things to be immediately intelligible and foreseeable. It is all that is inscribed in the relationship of familiarity with the familiar environment.[14] Every agent subjected to the same learning process will implicitly learn what is reasonable and unreasonable conduct and will share a common sense of limits and of the legitimate transgression of limits.

It is this common sense that constrains the list of relevant facts to be considered in sentencing. Unless considerations internal to the practice of sentencing suggest otherwise, the colour of the accused's hair, or whether she has a dog or a bird as a pet, or whether he is positioned exactly two inches closer or further from the judge in trial will not be relevant. That such considerations stand in need of justification does not derive from an indeterminacy in the rules of sentencing. An explicit list of all such irrelevancies would go on indefinitely and would itself be irrelevant. The irrelevancy of such considerations comes from a shared background that allows participants to anticipate the range of acceptable variation. This background explains our general agreement about how to go on, explains how it is that there are not disputes about every text, every reading of the text, and every conceivable gesture, event, and detail.

If rules do not apply themselves but are constrained by the pattern of life that informs them, then the discretion allotted to judges in sentencing is no more problematic than rule-following in more codified bodies of law. Both the evidently contextual rule that sentence should "fit" the crime and its circumstances and the apparently a-contextual rules of the Criminal Code are imbedded in a practice. Both sets of rules, whether explicit and formulaic or implicit and informal, will need to be interpreted in light of the relevant circumstances. Both are stabilized by an inferential, non-formulaic background understanding of what it is to follow the rule appropriately. What determines whether an activity is constrained is not whether it is or can be formulated but whether it makes sense to say of it that there is a right and a wrong way of proceeding.

Sentencing is just one particular example of the paradox of rules that plagues civil law as well as criminal law, common law as well as codified law, written law as well as oral law. More precision and detail is presumed to eradicate all uncertainty about how the rule is to be followed. "The principles of sentencing are roughly the following ..." seems to provide virtually no direction. We are under the impression that there is a single ideal of exactness and formality in law that is required before we can say we have a coherent legal system. But is this true?

Wittgenstein laid out the bewitching allure of a universal standard of exactness in a dialogue with his imaginary interlocutor:

If I tell someone "Stand roughly here" – may not this explanation work perfectly? And cannot every other one fail too?

But isn't it an inexact explanation? – Yes; why shouldn't we call it "inexact"? Only let us understand what "inexact" means. For it does not mean "unusable". And let us consider what we call an "exact" explanation in contrast with this one. Perhaps something like drawing a chalk line round an area? Here it strikes us at once that the line has breadth. So a colour-edge would be more exact. But has this exactness still got a function here: isn't the engine idling? And remember too that we have not yet defined what is to count as overstepping this exact boundary; how, with what instruments, it is to be established. And so on.

... "Inexact" is really a reproach, and "exact" is praise. And that is to say that what is inexact attains its goal less perfectly than what is more exact. Thus the point here is what we call "the goal". Am I inexact when I do not give our distance from the sun to the nearest foot, or tell a joiner the width of a table to the nearest thousandth of an inch?[15]

This response to the desire for more detail in law asks whether the goal of the exercise is served by greater precision. Some forms of precision (such as a list of all conceivable irrelevancies) may leave the engine idling.

This is not to say that more precision is always redundant. Some practices require us to give our distance from the sun to the nearest foot. Some bodies of law may require a continual refinement of terms and explicit constraints to be responsive to the kinds of human behaviour to which it is directed. But this articulation is not a standard for all other forms of law. The kinds of human behaviour towards which sentencing is directed and the conception of human beings to which it speaks may require less formalization rather than more. The precision required by different legal practices will depend on the purpose being fulfilled, and this is not a legal question but a moral or political or practical one.

There is a potential mischief in remarking that law is imbedded in practices that give it meaning and intelligibility. It may be true to remark, as Bourdieu does, that "every established order tends to produce ... the naturalization of its own arbitrariness," that the intelligibility of rules would be incomprehensible to one untrained in their use.[16] This general recognition of the fundamental arbitrariness of a legal system might suggest that law is no more than practice, that the rules of law are irrelevant. This conclusion fails to account for the fact that our training is also a training *in the rules*. This training in the rules is what lends legal systems their degree of autonomy, resilience, and internal coherence.

Locating the intelligibility of legal rules within social practices does not reduce them to practice. The forms of human life are there as a given, but within a form of human life, not *anything* counts as going on in the same way. Similarly, from a different perspective, maps arbitrarily adopt a point of view – but more scrupulous attention to an area brings prior maps, *devoted to the same inquiry*, into line. From the point of view of an outsider, inuksuit may be heaps of rocks or art objects; but within the hunting practices which make use of them as inuksuit, they guide behaviour, and one can read their directions correctly or incorrectly. Making law the subject of ethnographic inquiry brings out not its arbitrariness so much as, to quote Geertz, "the degree to which its meaning varies according to the pattern of life by which it is informed."[17]

Bearing in mind the distinctiveness of a training in legal rules, this linking of law to a larger background understanding nonetheless amounts to seeing law as more than a set of rules. It amounts to perceiving law as a whole outlook, as a dimension of social perception. The different interpretive and imaginative possibilities in the shared practices of a culture will structure particular legal understandings. Reflecting upon how a culture uses and conceptualizes a legal system will suggest ways of contemplating life as a whole, ways of defining relations between human beings. Clearly, however, not every society is imbued with the same sense of the legitimate and illegitimate transgression of limits.

Understanding the ways in which different societies imagine a socially legitimate sense of limits has been hindered by a sharp dichotomy in legal theory between law and custom. This opposition runs through a range of characterizations of non-state societies, whether they are cast as primitive and barbarous or romanticized as gentler and more human. On the former version, the passage to nation state is a neutral shift to the territorial principle and public law, from status to contract. On the latter, the movement from custom to law consists in the destruction of a natural order based on relational and reciprocal bonds. Law is symptomatic of the emergence of the state, and the state is an alienated form of society. The opposition at the root of these characterizations is fuelled by the idea that legal systems consist in sets of articulated rules which constrain human practices, a network of signposts which replaces more familiar and habitual conceptions of the social territory.

On this version of law, custom operates at a different quantum level than law. Custom is social morality and normativity, law is custom reformed and promoted. For custom to be accommodated within the state legal system, it would need to be rationalized by the standard of exactness set by western law. It would need to be made explicit and written into codified texts, restatements, and judicial decisions. This code of customary law could be recurred to in the settlement of disputes, aided by Native translators, both linguistic and cultural. That the spirit of customary law is destroyed in such a process has been interpreted as the consequence of the fundamental antinomy of law and custom, leading some authors to speculate whether "customary laws ... ought not, more properly, to form the subject of anthropological rather than legal research."[18]

There is, however, another way of reading the awkward fit between local ways of defining legitimate relations between human beings and the particular form of system and certainty aspired to in western law. Rather than opposing law to custom, both explicit and implicit rules are testimony to what Clifford Geertz has called a legal sensibility that makes intelligible and constrains the use of the rules. Western law's destruction of the spirit of customary law derives not from an opposition between rules and habits but from a lack of fit between the habitual practices of one society and those of another.

This analysis suggests that separating the field of inquiry into legal and anthropological research is wrong-headed. It also makes it less clear what we are looking for when we do legal – as opposed to strictly anthropological – research with non-state societies. If formalized rules do not define the necessary and sufficient conditions for the existence of a legal order, then how many other features of western law can be abandoned in the search for the *same* thing in a different society? If the characteristics of western law are too particular to be invoked as a standard, then how are we to test whether another society has the concept of law, but just in a different form, or whether it does not have it at all? What is law if it cannot, once and for all, be defined?

FAMILY RESEMBLANCES

Consider the term "lemon" for example. Lemons normally have certain characteristics: a yellow color when ripe, skin of a certain thickness with a waxy texture, ovoid shape, acid taste, a size and hardness that falls within a certain range, and so on. If an object has all these properties, it is definitely a lemon; but something which lacks one or more of them may still be a lemon. It might happen that in a particular region of the world, due to atomic fallout, lemon trees started producing fruit of a pinkish color and with a sweet taste, but having all the other characteristics of ordinary lemons. These fruits would doubtless still be lemons: pink lemons, or sweet pink lemons. A thing cannot lack all, or even very many, of the typical lemon properties, and still be lemon; but there is no one property, or group of two or three properties, which an object must have to be properly called a lemon. It must simply have some combination of the cluster of properties which lemons typically have. Thus lemons, like games, have no essence; and "lemon," like "game," has no unitary meaning.   G. Pitcher, *The Philosophy of Wittgenstein*[19]

David and Brierley, in their book on the major legal systems of the world, remark that "the idea of a 'legal family' does not correspond to a biological reality: it is not more than a didactic device."[20] This suggests that it might be better to understand the purposes for grouping characteristics of legal systems together rather than attributing metaphysical status to the concept of law. Perhaps it is not necessary to construct a list of necessary and sufficient conditions for the existence of legal orders. Rather than approaching the field with a definition, we might "look and see" what we call legal systems in different societies, setting boundaries for didactic purposes. This was Wittgenstein's manner of proceeding when he invited us to "look and see" whether there is anything common to what we call "games."

Wittgenstein's investigations into the concept "game" were an attempt to disabuse us of our craving for unity, not only in the more elementary concept of "game," but in general. We assume there has to be something in common with all games in the same way as we assume there must be something common to all legal systems. Although we can tolerate diversity on the fringes, we feel there must be some core essence or else we have not got a concept at all.

To disabuse us of these assumptions, Wittgenstein invited us to examine the individual instances to which a term applies, to see whether there is indeed something common to all, and whether there need be in order to be able to use general terms meaningfully. He was fighting against the "contemptuous attitude to the particular case," the notion that general terms must have necessary and sufficient criteria that constitute the essence of that term. If specific instances of general terms did not have common attributes, goes the argument, they would not be nameable by the single general term. There must be something common to all legal systems, or else they wouldn't all be called "legal systems." Wittgenstein attempted to show that this compulsion to find binding definitions is misguided – and also, that it is unnecessary.

The temptation to insist that there is one thing, or one set of things, in which law consists is analogous to the notion that there is one thing which is common to games. Wittgenstein invites us to examine this assumption:

Consider for example the proceedings that we call "games". I mean board-games, card-games, ball-games, Olympic games, and so on. What is common to them all? – Don't say: "There *must* be something common, or they would not be called 'games'" – but *look and see* whether there is anything common to all. –

For if you look at them you will not see something that is common to *all*, but similarities, relationships, and a whole series of them at that. To repeat: don't think, but look! – Look for example at board-games, with their multifarious relationships, Now pass to card-games; here you find many correspondences with the first group, but many common features drop out, and others appear. When we pass next to ball-games, much that is common is retained, but much is lost. – Are they all "amusing"? Compare chess with noughts and crosses. Or is there always winning and losing, or competition between players? Think of patience. In ball games there is winning and losing; but when a child throws his ball at the wall and catches it again, this feature has disappeared. Look at the parts played by skill and luck; and at the difference between skill in chess and skill in tennis. Think now of games like ring-a-ring-a-roses; here is the element of amusement, but how many other characteristic features have disappeared! And we can go through the many, many other groups of games in the same way; can see how similarities crop up and disappear.[21]

Engaging in this exercise with law can be illuminating. We are invited to *look and see* whether there is anything common to all of the various things that we call law. Is there something in common between civil law and common law? Between contract law and criminal law? What is familiar between statutory law and common law? What stands in for the law of remedies in civil law? What does the law of remedies share with this something? Consider usage in commercial law: what does commercial usage have in common with conventions in constitutional law? What do they both have in common with *law* in constitutional law? What does usage and convention in domestic law have to do with customary law in the field of international law? What do these concepts have in common or in disjunction with the law of Aboriginal rights?

If we *look and see*, we notice that there is not one thing that runs through all of these instances. Similarities crop up and disappear. If we look and see what the concept of law consists in, we will not see something that is common to all, "but similarities, relationships, and a whole series of them at that."

The notion of "law" has no unitary meaning, any more than the notion of a game has one unitary meaning. There may be groups of characteristics that indicate what we mean by different types of laws or legal systems. What is required is that they have *some* of the cluster of characteristics to qualify for what we mean by law, not all of them. And they need not be the *same* group of characteristics in each case, just as chess will exhibit some characteristics of a game but not necessarily at all the same ones as tennis or solitaire. And there is no way of specifying ahead of time and in the abstract just how much of a certain cluster of characteristics such as "formalized rules," "institutions," or "methods and procedures" is enough for something to qualify as a legal system.

But if there is no unitary meaning to the concept "law," then does this mean that there is no reason to talk of law as a general term? Does the concept have any meaning at all? Wittgenstein invoked the idea of "family resemblances" to show that although there is no essential definition of a general term, there are reasons for applying a single general term to a range of different things. What we perceive after the exercise of looking and seeing are "a complicated network of similarities overlapping and criss-crossing: sometimes overall similarities, sometimes similarities of detail. ... I can think of no better expression to characterize these similarities than 'family resemblances'; for the various resemblances between members of a family: build, features, colour of eyes, gait, temperament, etc., etc. overlap and criss-cross in the same way. – And I shall say: 'games' form a family."[22] Similarly, sometimes a characteristic of one form of law will be missing from another, but they will share some other characteristics. These other characteristics may be missing from a third form of law, but there will be overlaps with a fourth body of law which shares features with the second.

Law is not the sum of all of these parts, in the same way that a lawn is not the sum of all its blades of grass. You cannot just add or subtract from a general concept as though it is the sum of the individual related concepts. Subtracting the net and ball from tennis and adding cards and three players yields neither tarot nor modified tennis. Similarly, state-administered customary law is not custom merely codified and institutionalized, just as football is not tennis with teams.

There is an anxiety accompanying this understanding of general concepts that amounts to a fear that there is no certainty, no way of knowing in advance what counts and what does not. The use of the word "law," for example, would be unregulated, and what we mean by it, arbitrary. If the concept "law" is not circumscribed, then we don't really know what we mean by "law." Wittgenstein had a number of responses to this anxiety. Some of them speak to our dread that without absolute limits, we cannot speak meaningfully of a concept. Some of them show us what it means to use a concept meaningfully without reference to a unifying rule.

The first set of responses is affiliated with the earlier anxiety that an enclosure with a hole in it is as good as none. Wittgenstein has demonstrated how very often we in fact have unbounded concepts that function perfectly well. The concept "law" is not everywhere circumscribed by rules, "but no more are there any rules for how high one throws the ball in tennis, or how hard; yet tennis is a game for all that and has rules too."[23] This response is meant to show us that we are tempted to believe that we cannot use a concept unless we can use it with certainty, as though certainty had one unflagging standard. We have varying standards for certainty and exactness, and the standard in one context may not be the same in a second. It may serve no function in the second. Yet we function perfectly well with terms that would be vague in another setting. Indeed, the vagueness may be precisely what we are searching for with some concepts. Anything else would be redundant, or part of some other language game. "One might say that the concept 'game' is a concept with blurred edges. – 'But is a blurred concept a concept at all?' – Is an indistinct photograph a picture of a person at all? Is it even always an advantage to replace an indistinct picture by a sharp one? Isn't the indistinct one often exactly what we need?"[24]

The idea that each practice will evolve its own criteria for exactness speaks to the second set of responses that Wittgenstein had to the anxiety that there is no certainty in the use of a general concept. This is the idea that "we can draw a boundary – for a special purpose."[25] We can *make* the meaning of a general term unitary by specifying what its limits will be for a particular purpose. We might say that, for our purposes, nothing will count as a game unless it involves skill. And this boundary may be useful for certain things we want to do with it. Saying that 1 pace = 75 cm. may make the measure of a pace more usable for certain purposes.[26]

In the same manner, it may be useful to say that, for our purposes, all legal systems share features such as formalized rules, institutions, methodologies and procedures, a theory of legitimate authority, and a political tradition. We may use this schema as a didactic device in order to be able to see certain commonalities and dissimilarities between particular families of legal systems. There may well be instances where these boundaries are not drawn accurately and have excluded what we want to call a legal system. But there may not be. If what we are doing is, for example, comparing civil and common law traditions with socialist law, these boundaries may be accurate and instructive. We can create a list of common features of legal systems to make accurate historical statements about what distinguishes, for example, the sources of socialist law from the sources of civil law. However, the concept "law" is not unusable without those criteria (except for those special purposes) "no more than it took the definition: 1 pace = 75 cm. to make the measure of length 'one pace' usable."[27]

This point that a boundary can be drawn for a special purpose is linked to the idea that understanding what law is amounts to getting a grasp on what we call law, how we use the word. Why do we call something a law or a legal system? "Well, perhaps because it has a – direct – relationship with several things that have hitherto been called laws; and this can be said to give it an indirect relationship to other things we call the same name."[28] The way we use a concept now is connected with how we learned to use the concept in the past. We did not learn what a law was by being given a single unifying definition of law. If we are specifically trained in law, we were shown the ways that different laws operated, instances of how courts and legislatures treated statutes and prior cases, comparisons of the way certain bodies of law were related to each other, shown the historical connections and derivations of certain laws. Most tellingly, we were given cases, the standard method of legal education in North America being the case method, basing critical analysis on a collection of judicial decisions. For the most part, law is taught not by citing general rules but by providing an endless stream of examples. How do I know that there is a constitutional principle that is violated by a particular piece of legislation or that my clients would not succeed if they took their case to court? "It would be an answer to say, 'I have studied law.'"[29]

This understanding or knowledge of the law does not amount to an unformulated definition of the law which needs merely to be articulated in order that I recognize it as the expression of my knowledge.[30] This would be the equivalent of saying that I can have a mental picture of what law is that does not show me any particular law, just what is common to all laws. Not only is this picture a "bewitchment of our intelligence by means of our language," but it is not necessary. We learned how to use the concept with neither formulated nor unformulated definitions, by being given examples of various kinds of laws, showing how other laws can be constructed on the analogy of these; by being shown this or this which would scarcely be included among laws; and so on.[31] There is not some unarticulated rule underlying this learning that we were meant to grasp, nor need there be.

While general terms do not have unitary meanings, neither do they have fixed meanings, even in those practices associated with a fair degree of rigour. For example, science *gives* concepts circumscribed and unitary meanings. But these meanings should not be considered final and unalterable. What are understood to be the core and unchanging essence or definition of things such as, for example, science can change as new facts are discovered and new theories are put forward to explain those facts. Similarly, "lemon" may change its core meaning if atomic fallout on a South Seas island creates sweet pink lemons. Similarly, legal concepts that were once settled and rarely contested may undergo a shift in meaning. For example, the property tort of nuisance underwent a doctrinal shift in the late nineteenth century from strict liability to negligence and fault-based liability. And legal concepts that were once contested, such as the division of powers between provinces and the federal government in sections 91 and 92 of the 1867 British North America Act, may settle into the standards against which current constitutional dilemmas are resolved. The fixed meaning of terms might better be described on analogy with axes: "I do not explicitly learn the propositions that stand fast for me. I can *discover* them subsequently like the axis around which a body rotates. This axis is not fixed in the sense that anything holds it fast, but the movement around it determines its immobility."[32] The meaning of a term can be fixed by the purpose for which it is used, but this does not attach the term to something beyond the purpose for which it is used.

While concepts have no unitary meaning, we can put boundaries around them to use them for a purpose. These boundaries create what we mean by the term. They fix the meaning of a term for a purpose. But this fixity does not attach it to something beyond the purpose for which it is used. Once we have a clearer picture about the movement that immobilizes our concept of law, we have a sense both of its contingency and its necessity. This does not mean, however, that words have no meaning. They have the meaning that is given them by what they are used for. What would we be looking for if we were looking for meaning beyond this use?

This point can be illustrated with Wittgenstein's comments on one of his primitive language games: "'I set the brake up by connecting up rod and lever.' – Yes, given the whole rest of the mechanism. Only in conjunction with that is it a brake-lever, and separated from its support it is not even a lever; it may be anything, or nothing."[33] Things and words get their particular meaning from the use that is made of the object by the whole rest of the mechanism. Once it is employed as a brake-lever, however, it is neither anything nor nothing. If we wanted to teach what a brake-lever was, we would show not just the object (for the object alone could be a bookend, an art object, a sample of a kind of metal, a useless object ...) but how brake-levers are used in a variety of mechanisms. We may not know more about what a brake-lever is than this. But we may not need to know. It never troubled us before when we used brake-levers, or when we taught someone how to use them.

We can extend this notion of what it is to understand the concept "law" to legal anthropology. The hermeneutic problem in legal anthropology is to explain to people in another culture what a law is when we are not at all certain they have something analogous that will converge with our understanding. Following Wittgenstein, we would describe different laws to them, and we might add: This *and similar things* are called "laws." And we might ask pointedly: "And do we know any more about it ourselves?"[34]

We do not have a mental picture of law that transcends the particular examples of law, nor do we need it to use the concept. Neither do we need a unitary definition of law in order to be able to begin to recognize it in other cultures. Surely the process of discovery is more like this: I describe to someone from another culture the various kinds of things that we call law. I try to make my description as rich as possible. I include things that might not have been considered law fifty years ago but now are. I talk about things that were regarded as legal practice centuries ago but no longer count. I indicate that these other practices might be considered law if they only had this and this feature. I indicate that we, in our society, scarcely include this or that as laws.

In carrying on in this way, the other may indicate that what we call this kind of law is analogous to that aspect of his or her culture. They use similar grounds for excluding this and this from what they may, by analogy, call "law." They may be surprised that this particular something is considered "law" in our society, given that we have told them that for us, law can be a venerable category, for that is reviled as a form of alienation in their own. And so on.

This process of translation can be a lengthy process. We may mistake a "convergence of vocabularies for convergence of views."[35] This misapprehension may persist for a long time. On the other hand, the cultural translation of some aspects of a legal sensibility may be a very swift process. I may understand immediately what someone means once I have understood that person's language. There will be no criteria in advance for whether I have understood something or not, although we may develop signs or criteria for when a mistake has been made.

This is a process of refining the concept by giving examples. And do we know more about the meaning of "law" ourselves? We do not have unchanging criteria for correctness of fit in advance of the dialogue in which we engage. This whole exercise takes place without the benefit of a definition of law. We do not need an absolute list of necessary and sufficient criteria before we begin. We need a grasp of how we use the word in our culture.

This approach raises some questions, however – questions about the possibility for communication between cultures, about the possibility of distinguishing convergences of vocabularies from convergences of views. If the criteria for making a mistake and getting it right come from the habitual practices of distinct normative or cultural orders, then how might one make a claim to truth or certainty when habitual practices are not shared?

INTERCULTURAL COMMUNICATION

In *James Bay and Northern Québec: Ten Years After,*[36] Sylvie Vincent gives a brief account of the various cultural-historical routes that converged on each other in the James Bay Development Project. She begins by an exposé of the socioeconomic and political situation in Québec preceding the project and follows it with a description of the situation of the Cree and Inuit of Northern Québec. The accounts of the struggles of French Québec on the one hand and the Inuit of Nunavik on the other are both sympathetically rendered. She leaves the impression of two peoples simultaneously engaged in a vitally important quest for control and self-sufficiency, each cocooned by their cultural and political drives from perceiving the magnitude of difference between them.

Each culture articulates the world from the rhetoric of insiders and outsiders to the culture. Common historical reference points are interpreted according to the terms of each group. Hence the transfer of jurisdictional powers over Nouveau-Québec from the federal to provincial government is seen by one group as a wresting of control from an overwhelming continental linguistic majority, while the same event is perceived by the other as a suspicious move by a "little government."[37] It is in this spirit that Vincent cites Paul Veyne, who remarks that "historians construct plots, which each maps out like routes across a wholly objective field of events ... no historian can describe the entire field, because a route must have a course and cannot be everywhere: none of these routes is the true one, none is History."[38]

Respective histories of the land are based on seemingly groundless assumptions which are part of a whole, complex way of life. Among the assumptions invisibly woven into each way of life, some may contradict those of the other way of life. Both histories are more or less internally coherent but do not necessarily lend themselves to a shared coherence that would constitute some description of the entire field, some true account ... History.

The groundless, unquestioned beliefs that sustain a practice lend meaning to particular gestures, things, moments. If they were altered even slightly, they could sustain a completely different practice. It is possible to imagine, for example, a science based on the groundless assumption that things just disappear into thin air. Norman Malcolm paints a picture of what the society around such a science would look like. He conceives of those people as acting and thinking differently from ourselves in such ways as the following:

If one of them could not find his wallet, he would give up the search sooner than you or I would; also he would be less inclined to suppose that it was stolen. In general what we would regard as convincing circumstantial evidence of theft those people would find less convincing. They would take fewer precautions to protect their possessions against loss or theft. They would have less inclination to save money, since it too can just disappear. They would not tend to form strong attachments to material things. They would stand in a looser relation to the world that we do. The disappearance of a desired object, which would provoke us to a frantic search, they would be more inclined to accept with a shrug. Of course their scientific theories would be different; but also their attitude toward experiment, and inference from experimental results, would be more tentative. If the repetition of a familiar chemical experiment did not yield the expected result, this *could* be because one of the chemical substances had vanished.[39]

Malcolm uses this example to equate the groundlessness of scientific belief with the groundlessness of religious belief. The legitimacy of each entire activity is not amenable to proof in the same way that it is not possible to imagine what would prove or disprove the assumption that things disappear into thin air, what would count as evidence one way or the other. Both activities rest on leaps of faith. In order to understand each activity, the fundamental beliefs of each community must be understood, as well as the way of life of each.

We can imagine what might happen when two communities with fundamentally different ways of interpreting the world come into contact with each other. Fundamental differences in outlook may be imposed by the more powerful upon the other. Or, indeed, fundamental differences may go undetected as each group reads the other in only familiar terms. The way in which Inuit people and Qallunaat people interact with children illustrates this cross-cultural misfiring. The fact that I can give an account of this difference also suggests something about intercultural communication.

Inuit children are often given the names of respected people in the community. If you are named after another person, that person calls you *Saunik*, which means: of my bone, or part of me. A child named after an adult also calls him or her *Saunik*. It is believed that the elder inhabits that child once the elder has died. Because the child is inhabited by the spirit of the elder, it would be inappropriate to order the child around or to direct the child's activities, just as it would be disrespectful to control an elder's behaviour. Inuit children are thus given a wide berth of discretion in their behaviour. They are presumed to learn by their mistakes in the same way as an adult would. Just as it would be considered rude to give unsolicited advice and direction to an adult, so it would be to these children, inhabited by the spirits of adults.

This is not the way that Qallunaat perceive children and their needs. This is not the conceptual foundation of the Qallunaat family and other child-oriented institutions, which assumes that children require structure in order to thrive. Children are constantly monitored, directed, and redirected. There is a rich colloquial and professional vocabulary for parents who do not set sufficient limits on their children's behaviour, most of it pejorative.

Working at Kuujjuaq's battered women's shelter in the summer of 1992, I noticed this difference in child-rearing styles. The shelter only sheltered Inuit women; the administration was predominantly Qallunaat. The Inuit women infrequently intervened spontaneously in what their children were doing. The Qallunaat workers were constantly pulling children off counters, telling them not to eat this or that, deciding it was time for the child to have a bath or to go to bed. Some of the Inuit women became self-conscious of the workers' intrusiveness and made an effort to direct their children, to avoid the almost palpable critique that came with such pointed interventions. The Qallunaat workers would often whisper among themselves that Inuit women never washed their children, that they showed reckless disregard for their needs, that they needed to to be taught how to parent. Alternatively, the Qallunaat were thought by the Inuit to be intrusive and interfering, unnecessarily controlling of the children, always offering unsolicited advice.

Because each orientation to the world is rooted in groundless assumptions, in a whole way of life, there is no metaphysical reference point to which one can refer to claim that one orientation accurately reflects the nature of children. Qallunaat women have a way of construing Inuit women's behaviour and vice versa. Compounding this, Inuit tend less to directly tell an adult what to do and are anxious to avoid appearing to give advice. Social control is more often handled through gossip. Qallunaat are not often competently attuned to the nuances of Inuit gossip. Alternatively, offering unsolicited advice is not considered inappropriate amongst Qallunaat, especially among the professional and bureaucratic classes making up the majority of Qallunaat residents in Kuujjuaq. Both groups remain immunized from the other's frame of reference.

In the face of the apparent determinism of discourse, it is difficult to conceive of there being communication across cultures. There is a feeling that even if we have managed to translate words (indeed, most Inuit of Nunavik share English or French with the Qallunaat), we need some way of translating the view of reality that stands behind language. Otherwise we will end up ricocheting reinterpretations indefinitely off each other as one culture assesses another culture's critique with its own.

Related to the idea that our ways of understanding the other are projections of our ways of understanding ourselves is the intimation that cross-cultural value judgments are suspect from the outset. Rorty sets up the recognition that our central beliefs may be no more necessary or natural than our "peripheral" and "cultural" ones in the following manner:

When we bourgeois liberals find ourselves thinking of people in this way – when, for example, we find ourselves reacting to the Nazis and the fundamentalists with indignation and contempt – we have to think twice. For we are exemplifying the attitude we claim to despise. We would rather die than be ethnocentric, but ethnocentrism is precisely the conviction that one would rather die than share certain beliefs ... we begin to wonder whether our attempts to get other parts of the world to adopt our culture are different in kind from the efforts of fundamentalist missionaries.[40]

Questions about cross-cultural communication are related to ones about value judgments across normative orders.

It is not clear, though, that the lack of a transcendentally neutral language, uncontaminated by the stake that each community has in its way of life, reduces the possibility of cross-cultural communication. Nor is it clear that the lack of metaphysical foundation implies that we are left with some vapid assertion that anything one group of people does is worthy of respect by another, or with empty tag-ons such as "and bourgeois liberal democracies are best." Both the pursuit of foundations and relativism fail to capture the development of understanding between cultures and the nature of critiques of ethnocentrism.

Just as solipsism has no currency as between the I's and you's of "our" social world, it has no currency between the we's and them's of different cultural worlds. Doubts about the other arise within shared practices of doubting and taking things for granted. Just as doubting whether a term has the same meaning for another person only makes sense in the context of a shared habitual repertoire, doubting whether we have understood another culture also only makes sense in the context of an intercultural repertoire shared between we's and them's. Criteria for ethnocentrism are given in the intercultural practices in which we have been trained to communicate cross-culturally.

In articulating the notion of fundamental differences between communities, we make reference to things that are comprehensible in our community. We understand and can picture what it would be to use objects in an aesthetic way as opposed to as part of a machine. We understand what is meant by the phrase "disappear into thin air." Although the Qallunaat in Kuujjuaq may not have originally perceived the difference, the Inuit way of viewing children and of interacting with them can be made comprehensible to them. It was made at least marginally comprehensible to me.

Even articulating the problem assumes a common ground on which differences can be pointed out. The image of a convergence of vocabularies without a convergence of views is only comprehensible because there are *some* shared practices, if minimally the practice of translation. To even talk of a cross-cultural misinterpretation indicates that there is a shared way of determining a mistake. In this event, not all signs have been misinterpreted.

Correcting cross-cultural misunderstandings, then, is not a metaphysical exercise. It is something inherent in the ways that we communicate with one another. Just as there is an habitual repertoire for things like map-making, there is an habitual repertoire for cross-cultural dialogue.

This cross-pollinated repertoire is not a matter of opinion but of understanding. It is also not a matter of consensus or agreement. It is the background understanding that must be in place in order for disagreements and consensus to get off the ground. Just as mathematicians do not verify that the numbers have not shifted on the page each time they make a calculation, so the common ground of cross-cultural disagreements is assumed in negotiations between cultures. This common ground is wider than is thought; indeed, it is wider than is thinkable. It is the limit of our visual field.

This focus on an intercultural common ground is different than the concept of formal equality. It does not presume some neutral standard, outside of each practice, which is the measurement of sameness. If there is transcendence of local history, it is as an extension of local history through contest and incorporation. The original position is not abandoned for an impartial, general point of view: it is elaborated to include an understanding of the ways that partial points of view affect other partial points of view.

Such an understanding of cross-cultural communication does not provide independent ways of determining when true communication has taken place, of adjudicating between contending normative orders. Nor does it tell us what to do in any actual situation where we may find ourselves unable to achieve understanding. An intercultural repertoire develops in a way analogous to how someone might learn to connect a rod and lever to form a brake-lever. We are trained in the use of certain forms of questioning, certain styles of listening. Standards about how to proceed are given in the practice. We evaluate what other people do at the same time as we learn what it is they do. Hence the notion that we could lay some all-purpose blanket of respect over all human behaviour voids the concept of respect of any meaning. Respect is affiliated with understanding.

The processes at work in the emergence of cross-cultural understanding can be illustrated with the example of adoption among the Inuit.[41] Traditional adoptions are a common practice among the contemporary Inuit. A relative of the mother will indicate that he or she wants the child once it is born. It is understood that the request will be honoured, and for a mother to decline would require a considerable degree of personal fortitude. These adoptions do not respect provincial adoption laws. There is no prior home visit or evaluation by a social worker. The Canadian legal standard of the "best interests of the child" is not invoked.

Recently, the number of adoptions that occur within the provincial legal norm has increased. According to one of the lawyers performing "official" adoptions in Nunavik, traditional adoptions are not legally binding in court.[42] They can be successfully contested by, for example, a mother who did not give consent according to provincial standards. In other words, the traditional practice is, according to the court, a social practice, not a legal one.

The arguments this lawyer marshalled to justify the paramountcy of provincial law included the idea that traditions are not frozen in time and that the needs of the Inuit have changed to justify the priority of provincial norms – Inuit needs are now the same as Qallunaat needs. The lawyer also felt that the practice of traditional adoption would not be harmed by the intervention of social workers, the standard of the "best interests of the child," and provincial consent standards. These latter procedures were conceived as value- and culture-neutral.

An argument could be made that in fact a whole web of relations between the Inuit could be altered by these changes to traditional adoptions in the same way that the belief that things disappear into thin air could have ramifications for a multiplicity of social practices. Elaborate kin relations bearing on innumerable aspects of the Inuit way of life could be modified. To give one example, whereas traditional adoption might have ensured elders they would be cared for in their old age, this insurance could be attenuated by the primacy of the best interests of the child. Further, as most Kujjuamiut have at least one such adopted sibling, the whole concept of the family, of kin, and of who is responsible for the care of children stands to be altered when official adoptions supplant traditional ones.

What is perhaps less visible in this transformation is that the itinerant court in Nunavik tends to take into account the Inuit context in which "official" adoption determinations are made. Hence a sixty-six-year-old woman was granted adoption of a two-month-old child, an arrangement which, in the South, would have likely failed the evaluation stage, let alone a tribunal hearing. One might just as easily say of the legal tradition of provincial adoption that it is not frozen in time and space. The "best interests of the child" standard is not a rule that applies itself; it gains its coherence by taking into account divergent criteria in divergent contexts.

This case was not necessarily warmly embraced in the community as a sign of positive flexibility in the provincial standard. The two Inuit with whom I stayed in Kuujjuaq were perturbed by the case. They knew the adoptive mother and felt strongly that she was too old to care for an infant and that her motives were not drawn from a generous spirit. The culturally sensitive aspirations of the court may not be producing outcomes beneficial to Inuit children. Another layer of intercultural complexity arises.

One could adopt an attitude of distress at the loss of a vital part of Inuit culture. One could also be relieved that Inuit children and birth parents are being spared some of the more harmful effects of traditional adoption. One might approve of a flexible reading of the "best interests" standard as a culturally sensitive adaptation. One might also critique a flexible reading as an overly naive attempt to accommodate culture at the expense of the deeper psychological needs of the Inuit.

Alternatively, the provincial practice might simply be applied without this order of reflection or interpretation about its worth. The non-Aboriginal standard is used in precisely such an unreflective manner in hundreds of adoption cases a year. Similarly, traditional Inuit adoption is currently a standard practice engaged in with neither hesitation nor justification. In easy cases where there is no contestation between Inuit and non-Inuit adoption practices, the practice needs no further interpretation or examination. This is just what is done. In contested cases, the evaluation of either practice proceeds by the introduction of new narratives (the implications of this loss to other Inuit practices, the fate of a two-month-old adopted by a sixty-year-old) and by different forms of argument (e.g., exploiting the argument that cultures are not frozen). This is the nature of cross-cultural dialogue.

To understand the anxiety that the provincial standard could undermine a whole way of life is to begin to evaluate it. To understand the future predicaments of the then two-month-old child is to be pulled towards another view of the right thing to do. In this process, there is no global respect for what people are inclined to do. The rudimentary complexity of the narratives makes such innocuous open-mindedness naive.

If respect is something that comes with understanding, then what does it mean to treat the Inuit people with the same respect as the Qallunaat? What kind of accommodation is necessary to ensure that Inuit women and Qallunaat women are both treated fairly by the criminal justice system? How should institutions be designed to ensure that everyone, unique and different, is treated equally?

Richard Rorty depicts the tasks of a liberal democracy being divided between agents of love and agents of justice: "The former insist that there are people out there whom society has failed to notice. They make these candidates for admission visible by showing how to explain their odd behavior in terms of a coherent, if unfamiliar, set of beliefs and desires – as opposed to explaining this behavior with terms like stupidity, madness, baseness or sin. The latter, the guardians of universality, make sure that once these people are admitted as citizens, once they have been shepherded into the light by the connoisseurs of diversity, they are treated just like all the rest of us."[43] This neat distinction makes it seem as though the guardians of universality simply apply a standard of same-ness to objects *independently* grouped together for the *same kind* of dif-ference, as though the principle informing the groupings were not the desire to treat like objects alike. It also makes it seem as though the connoisseurs of diversity are informed about which differences are *rele-vant* for their scrutiny by the very objects themselves and not by the uses to which they want to put such contrasts.

In fact the agents of love insist upon certain differences because over-looking them would mean that the unique humanity of the subject is overlooked, something of general if not universal significance. Con-versely, the universality guarded by the agents of justice is diversity. The tasks are not, in fact, independent of one another.

The idea that the tasks are separable is reflected in an arrangement whereby an itinerant court, thick on rules and thin on context, flies into a community and conducts its hearings next to a healing circle, focused on the particularities of its Inuit participants with the question "what has hurt you?" – and there is no intercourse between the two.

The idea that the tasks are in fact inseparable would be reflected in a different kind of attention, a different kind of audience. This audience would be quite distinct from the traditional itinerant court and would place radically different demands on western court personnel. It would also be different from traditional Inuit legal practices. It would be a kind of syncretic mix of the two, born on an intercultural common ground. This syncretism is not inconceivable.

THE FAMILIARITY OF LAW

"This is what we do – so this is what you are going to do." This is not very different from the message conveyed to the Inuit by the Qallunaat justice system – from Binney's 1931 declaration of the "illegality" of Inuit law[44] to the judge on the June 1992 circuit who made it understood that there was to be no talking and no laughing in his court. This is a differ-ent message than that conveyed by sentencing circles which say some-thing more like the following: "This is what we would do in these circumstances [or, more realistically: 'you are already familiar with what we would do'] – now tell us what you would do."

The leading case on Canadian sentencing circles is *R. v. Moses* (1992).[45] At the end of trial, after the accused has been found guilty or has so pleaded, the judge, unorthodoxly, opens sentencing to members of the community, including the accused, the victim, and relatives of each. The circle also includes the police, judge, Crown counsel, and defence. The courtroom is physically rearranged so that all participants sit in a circle facing each other. Input ranging from information about the history of the accused and the victim to information about the community and court is invited from all participants. Recommendations are solicited about what would constitute an appropriate sentence. While all input is admissible and valued, the judge reserves the right to override the final consensus of the group. Sentencing circles are meant to elicit more Aboriginal participation in the justice system; the Nunavik circle was an attempt to put this process into motion in Québec.

Sentencing circles aspire to subvert the conceit that what one group of people does is, after all, only common sense. If juridical rules emerge from the recognized values in which the group feels at home, sentencing circles are a recognition that Canadian law may be strange and unfamil- iar to the people who first felt at home on the land.

One of the arguments of this book has been that the failure to be · compelled by certain descriptions is an indication that, whatever else one has acquired, one has not acquired the practice that so describes things. Among those of us who share a common practice, we can assume that our audience understands us, with no need of further justification. To hear a tale is to be moved. For human beings, similarly sensitized, some remarks require no further justification. They *are* a justification. Bedrock has been reached.

This would be similar for someone who, in an argument about a possible course of action, replied, "But that's against the law!" The way in which this remark is delivered and received is a symptom of learning. For one who has learned to use words and objects along with other people grouped around a common activity, the normative content of the statement *is* its factual content. That the course of action is, as a matter of fact, against the law is, as a matter of justice, persuasive. There is no positivistic temper to this kind of remark. The law is not binding because it has been pronounced by the state or because it can be enforced. It is binding because those who pronounce it are appealing to a common ground without which they would feel they could not find their feet in the other party's world.

The factual and normative content of the statement "But that's against the law" are not, however, inseparable. Sometimes pointing out that something is against the law is only a descriptive statement and not a normative one. "So what?" one might respond, and with reason. In these cases as well the law is not binding simply because it has been pronounced by the state, nor because it can be enforced. It fails to bind because all it has is force. Part of the ability of law to be legitimate flows from its ability to make people feel that the law to which they are reputed to be subject as a matter of fact is not strange and unfamiliar as a matter of heart.

How two distinct senses of the ordinary world should be reconciled so that spades turn on a common bedrock is a difficult question. Such a reconciliation would not mean there would be no more individuals with whom justifications come to an end, no more human beings for whom something other than persuasion – incarceration, for example – would be appropriate. Individuals will still be born into a world that is already ordered. In this world, it will still be true that, as Iris Murdoch put it, "I can decide what to say but not what the words mean which I have said. I can decide what to do but I am not master of the significance of my act."[46] Focusing attention on the significance of our actions will still require *obedience,* and in this manner, someone might still feel a sense of *tigujaumaju,* of being taken away by an uncontrollable force.

The feeling that accompanies this sad realization – the awareness of another human being's alienation – would be tempered by the shared significance Inuit and Qallunaat ascribe to actions. If Inuit and Qallunaat worlds were reconciled, the sorrow that accompanies the banishment of a human being would be attended by that much less of a sense that the world is an unjust place – tragic, indeed, but not unjust. Similarly, if men understood the daily reality of subjugation that many women take for granted, there would be fewer instances where a woman's primary response to the incarceration of a man was an immediate sense of relief.

Sentencing circles are not, then, exactly like healing circles. Both might deal with the same desperate acts. When the participants in a healing circle are asked what has hurt them, however, no one makes a comment, nobody says anything. If there is a demand for obedience it is the call to direct a just and loving gaze at the humanity of each participant. The main purpose of the circle is to liberate participants from their affliction.

In sentencing circles the community holds up a mirror to the offender. The offender may well speak about the history that led to his or her act. In sentencing circles, however, the community as a whole is also asked "What has hurt you?" The central aim of the circle is to liberate the community from the events that have brought it to this point. The answer from the community might well be: "You, the offender." Despite having bared his or her soul, an offender could be abandoned in a manner that would be cruel and unusual for a healing circle.

Sentencing circles are not like the traditional circuit court either. The traditional court is rarely sensitized to the ways that its commands are perceived locally. Not only is the court unaware of its impact in partic- ular cases, it is unaware of its overall weight, its history as told from the inside of the culture upon which it acts. In sentencing circles, the judge makes herself, her court, and her people vulnerable to a more uncom- fortable response to the question: "What has hurt you?" By inviting the community to speak, sentencing circles open up the possibility that the community – and the offender – might respond: "You have!"

The possibility for this response is contained in the circle's methodol- ogy. Not only are defence and Crown scored into a richer orchestration of voices: both counsel and court are further transformed into objects of narrative. As Barry Stuart, the presiding judge, remarked in the *Moses* case, for the traditional court, "Very little is known in sentencing about offenders, victims, the crucial underlying factors causing the criminal behaviour, or about the larger context of the home and community, and almost nothing is known about how the court process affects the conflict or upon [sic] the persons involved."[47] Making the court an object of Inuit accounts permits the Inuit to fill in this historiographical gap.

This transformation of the circuit court into an object of narrative could be seen in Nunavik's first sentencing circle. The first Inuit com- ment in the circle came from an elder woman who remarked, "Even if they send people down South, they are still with white people who have different languages. Even when they come back from down there there is no improvement. It is better if people with the same language and lifestyle try to help.

"I am happy the court is starting to do something. There are a lot of people who know how to help but then the accused go to court and are sentenced. They cannot go further as the Inuit cannot get involved."[48] What has been repressed – the Inuit accounting of Qallunaat sensibilities – is given a formal hearing for Qallunaat ears. What has been segregated as local gossip now penetrates the imagination of the court and forces upon it a more immediate reckoning.

The idea that the judge in a sentencing circle says "This what we would do – now tell us what you would do" makes his task seem analogous to the legal anthropologists searching out family resemblances between Inuit and Qallunaat legal sensibilities. A significant difference is that the court continues to ask the question in different settings, with different participants. There is no presumed authenticity, flagged by the moment ethnographers left the field, against which the contemporary Inuit are measured. Local Inuit determine and redetermine, discover and rediscover, who they are and who they are becoming – as do the Qallunaat participants.

Mary Crnkovich, who attended the Nunavik sentencing circle as an observer for Pauktuutit, raises the spectre of authenticity in a report she submitted on her observations:

There appears to be some confusion about Inuit-based justice initiatives and community-based justice initiatives. By virtue of Inuit being the majority within the community, does not necessarily make a community-based initiative an Inuit-based initiative. In fact, very few of the community-based initiatives are rooted in Inuit tradition. Adult diversion and circle sentencing are not Inuit traditions. In order for alternatives to be Inuit-based, Inuit must be allowed to design and implement them.

... [The sentencing circle] is but one alternative to the existing sentencing practice originating not within Inuit tradition but another aboriginal tradition.[49]

Imbedded within this criticism are several conceptions of the relationship between justice and culture. Some of them, I would contend, are legitimate. Others of them are not.

In her report, Crnkovich describes the almost complete lack of community participation in the decision to hold a sentencing and in the design of the circle. The court, as it has historically done, dropped into the community and within two hours haphazardly pulled the circle together without prior community organizing or consultation. The fact that the community was Inuit no more made such a parachuted initiative Inuit than the fact that the traditional itinerant court deals with Inuit offenders makes *it* Inuit. Local participation is essential to disclose a sensibility that has been absent, by now notoriously, from state-administered justice.

Crnkovich's comment, however, underlines the distinction between local Inuit initiatives and those that are not "rooted in Inuit tradition." That sentencing circles originated in another Aboriginal community, she suggests, compromises their ability to be specifically Inuit. But it is not clear what it would mean for something to be specifically Inuit. The notion of an authentic legal sensibility is like the idea that manufactured goods destroyed the Inuit economy, a notion that overlooks the fact that what makes something a local *good* is that it has a local *usage*. The way in which an initiative is appropriated and *used* by the Inuit – or indeed resisted – will be more telling about its authority than convergence with ancient accounts about the collectivity. The habitual return of the court to the question "What would you do in these circumstances?" gives it access to the ways that contemporary Inuit incorporate or resist things originally unfamiliar.

There are further questions about the legitimacy of sentencing circles. Two of the most pressing are: who is directing the process (and by what right), and who is being asked to participate? These questions come together in another of Mary Crnkovich's criticisms of the Nunavik circle. Crnkovich stresses above that legitimate alternatives to the traditional court must be designed and implemented by the Inuit. Subsequent remarks which qualify this position might appear to make her commendations about local control insincere, or at least ambivalent:

Within the Inuit community, this reconstruction must be done in a way that is appropriate for and includes all segments of the community. If alternatives simply allow for the transfer of the power of the judge to a select and powerful few in the community, little has been accomplished. Women have expressed concern about the introduction of Inuit traditions into the justice system without further examination and discussion because of their discriminatory nature against women ... An example of the concerns raised is the view of some elders regarding wife abuse. The view that wife abuse is not a serious crime or is the result of a woman's lack of obedience to her husband or non-acceptance of her traditional role is not one shared by many contemporary Inuit women. Yet this is a view that is heard expressed by elders. If elders are given responsibility for sentencing circles, which might better reflect Inuit tradition, there could be problems.[50]

These remarks seem paradoxical when juxtaposed against her earlier critique about the inauthenticity of the initiative. She seems to be simultaneously valorizing local Inuit control while expressing reservations about its legitimacy. This is perhaps especially peculiar in the light of other comments directed at a duplicity in the judge's solicitations in the sentencing circle. Crnkovich was perturbed by the fact that the judge reserved the right to disregard the circle's recommendations: "[R]eferring to the group's work as 'advice' yet telling them they are equal to the judge, presented a mixed message and [put into question] how 'equal' the members really were."[51]

The "concerns raised" about the views of some elders about wife abuse were not raised once in the sentencing circle nor were they raised by Inuit women during the course of Mary Crnkovich's stay in Community C. If women "expressed concerns" about the introduction of Inuit traditions into the justice system, they certainly weren't expressing them in the forum of the sentencing circle.

"So what?" part of me wants to add. Part of me wants to say that Crnkovich's anxieties about the safety of Inuit women are benevolent and just, whether they were given voice to in the circle or not. As the written judgment of the Nunavik circle itself indicates, violence against women is staggering in the North. Anthropological accounts indicate that most of the violence in traditional Inuit communities arose because of the abduction – the abduction – of women. Crnkovich did not need to hear in the forum of the sentencing circle general concerns about the safety of Inuit women to know that women in the Arctic are in just as precarious a situation *vis à vis* male dominance as they are in the South.

This is, as Mary Crnkovich notes, "a sensitive issue." She manoeuvers around her own (no doubt understandable) discomfort by suggesting that the issue must be "resolved by the Inuit before Inuit-based justice initiatives are incorporated into the justice system or community-based initiatives are redesigned to reflect Inuit traditions."[52] This also appears to be a peculiarly confused and ambivalent suggestion. She clearly does not mean that an adequate resolution could sanction the views of the elders she reproaches. Because she understands what those views meant for Inuit women, she cannot respect them. Control must be local and Inuit, as long as it is not handed over to those who have historically abused it.

Is this not the position of the judge, who declares that everyone is equal, unless they are fundamentally different than the judge? The ultimate sense of the illegitimate transgression of limits appears to be set by the Qallunaat. Are Mary Crnkovich and Judge Dutil just more sophisticated reincarnations of Binney who criminalized the Inuit way of dealing with conflict? Crnkovich, along with the judge, appears to want to get the Qallunaat out of the circle while simultaneously reserving a fairly central place for them. This seems like a pernicious piece of mystification. Or is it?

All of this is an oblique way of asking about the appropriate place of the Qallunaat in the North. And it is a way of inquiring into the judge's trump and of asking whether it can be exercised in the name of justice and not in the name of his or her own people's limited version of it. If it is only a version, then why, beyond the reflexes of imperialism, is the Inuit community's version not uncompromisingly accepted rather than potentially undermined by a trumping mechanism?

The seeming solipsism of this problem takes on a different complexion if our attention is focused on vulnerable groups within the community. One could easily imagine Inuit communities where battered women have no recourse to aid from local authorities such as the mayor. It is entirely conceivable that in communities of less than 1,400 inhabitants, local authorities might feel less inclined to come to a battered woman's assistance because they are related or otherwise attached to the offender. Indeed, the local authority *might well be* her abuser. To put this scenario in perspective, I want to salvage some material from my own fieldnotes from the Nunavik sentencing circle.

In the week following the circle, I interviewed Judge Dutil. I asked him whether he could play a role in the selection of the circle to ensure that prejudicial interests did not skew safe outcomes for women. He replied that he relied on the mayor of each community, in conjunction with the probation officer assigned to Nunavik, to secure those guarantees. He remarked that for the Nunavik circle, he had assigned responsibility to the probation officer for composition of the circle.[53]

Curious about how the group had been selected, I asked the probation officer to comment on how this particular circle had come about. He indicated that when he had been assigned the task of organizing the circle he delegated it to the mayor of the community. He justified this decision by remarking that it was not his community and that the task was "too political."[54]

What if that particular mayor was not an unqualified champion of the right of women to be free from violence? He could have exerted his influence in the circle in a way that perpetuated the vulnerabilities of women. Should we shrug our shoulder and say, with the probation officer, this is not our community – these are not our people – these are not our problems?

I would feel strongly, as I imagine would most of my readers, that if the mayor of Community C exerted his influence inadequately to protect a battered woman in the circle, the judge should render null the recommendations of the circle. Insensitivity to the daily realities of violence against women fails to appeal to a common ground on which women, too, must be made to feel at home.

This suggests that "the Inuit community"'s version of justice should not be uncompromisingly accepted because the Inuit community is not one unified thing. Personal, local, engaged, embodied knowledge is not of itself suspect. One would need to bring reasons to doubt local knowledge in the same way one would need to bring reasons to doubt that the traditional circuit court is effective in Nunavik. (Many such reasons have, of course, been brought to bear.) But local knowledge, like any other form of knowledge, is not sacrosanct and can be challenged by alternative facts and interpretations.

One of the reasons that local knowledge is not impervious to critique is that it is being constantly revised and, like the traditional Inuit economy, penetrated and cross-pollinated by realities originally outside (and now inside) its boundaries. The Inuit and Qallunaat are not two separate entities, solipsistically miscommunicating for the last several centuries: their ability to communicate, even their ability to speak to each other about misinterpretations, is grounded in an intercultural reality against which both peoples make sense of their own and the other's activities.

Another reason that local knowledge is not impervious to critique is that within the community knowledge is localized to different spaces and different ways of occupying those spaces. Grouping all of the Inuit together to remark on the sameness of their difference with the Qallunaat overlooks the fact that not all of their differences are the same. Some of the relevant differences among the Inuit – relevant to the task of guarding the diverse ways in which humanity expresses itself – have been submerged. The way in which Inuit women's humanity has been repressed by violence is illustrative. For Qallunaat officials to refuse to meddle in this state of affairs reinforces its normality. This is a covert way of meddling.

The judge's trump, then, is not unqualifiedly unjustified. There is some shared sense that there are no acceptable justifications for leaving women – Inuit or otherwise – in a position where their fear for their lives and integrity is not recognized and mitigated. If agreements have not settled around the judge's obligation to protect battered women, then the onus is on those who would contest it to bring arguments to bear. And cultural integrity cannot be invoked because the identification of culture with male practices is, as I have argued in the context of place-name maps, an assumption as arbitrary as the idea that objects might or might not disappear into thin air.

If local knowledge is not sacrosanct, however, then neither is the knowledge of the judge – knowledge informed by the familiar locales in which he lives out his life. In written reasons for judgment in Nunavik's first sentencing circle, Judge Dutil remarked that

of course the judge is not bound by the recommendations of the participants in the consultation ... It is understandable, however, that if the judge systematically set aside the circle's recommendations, it may become entirely useless to hold such sessions. In my opinion, the judge must listen to the participants, discuss with them if need be, listen to their recommendations and follow them in most instances, unless he has serious reasons to set them aside, in which case [he] must explain clearly the reasons for his decision, so that the sessions are not looked upon as futile exercises.[55]

This is as good an expression as any of the judge's trump in sentencing circles. Dutil is not suggesting that the trump is a matter of sheer fiat. It is not some version of the unilateral declaration "bourgeois liberal democracies are the best." When an impasse is reached between the judge and the circle, Dutil suggests that the way to proceed is rhetorical. But if his reasons have not swayed the circle, then it is hard to distinguish his manoeuver from a unilateral declaration. It is not clear why his interpretation becomes the rule. This asymmetry seems to be out of accord with the deliberative aspirations of sentencing circles.

As it now stands, a trumping judge would bring closure to the circle, declaring her reasons for so doing, as Dutil indicates is only appropriate. Currently, such a decision can only be appealed to a provincial court of appeal and subsequently to the Supreme Court of Canada. This structure also seems to remove the process further from an Aboriginal setting. If the judge is given the ability to bring closure and the case is then only appealable to an external arena that only includes people from her culture, there is no way of determining whether the judge has inadvertently stifled a perfectly legitimate Inuit concern. How much more likely are appeal-court judges to be alert to these sensibilities when they do not have even the fleeting acquaintance with Inuit culture that circuit-court judges acquire as they parachute in and out of Inuit communities?

Perhaps another way of framing this is to say that the legitimacy of the judge's trump in cases where women's vulnerabilities are not protected by the sentencing circle does not come from the judge, but from a familiarity with what violence does to women. The judge, in invoking closure, is the intermediary for this understanding. Someone else would have been justified in speaking out in the Nunavik circle, drawing attention to the inequities of treating battered Inuit women to less protection than their counterparts in the South. Indeed, someone else may have been justified in speaking out at the outset of the circle and calling its legitimacy into question on the understanding that battered women are highly unlikely to speak freely about their battering partner in his presence for fear of reprisals. Inviting a woman to speak out in these circumstances places her unconscionably in jeopardy. The very purpose of the circle – to elicit different understandings of what to do in the circumstances – is poisoned by this oversight. If the judge cannot sway this understanding of the experience of battered women, then indeed his trump looks like a unilateral declaration.

This begins to suggest a way to structure sentencing circles and appeals from sentencing circles. Recollect that Mary Crnkovich declined the judge's offer to participate in the Nunavik circle, feeling that this would be a presumptuous continuation of Qallunaat interference in Inuit communities. In any event, her politesse was largely ineffectual and contradictory. She was an *éminence grise* at the circle, moderately directing its outcome from offstage. She also wrote a report of the circle that was circulated amongst the Inuit as well as amongst various departments of justice. Judge Dutil read her report. People in the community, including the victim, read her report. Mary Crnkovich was embraced by the circle whether she wanted to be or not. What if she had raised her concerns about the safety of Inuit women at the outset of the circle?

If the judge had accepted her concerns, he could have invoked his trump to terminate the circle. Perhaps the accused, and others, may have had reasons to continue, may have felt cheated by this decision, even if the reasons for it were clearly explained. Certainly there were Inuit participants who were grateful for the opportunity to speak, an opportunity that would have been squelched by this manoeuver. On the other hand, if the judge had overridden Mary Crnkovich's concerns, she would have been stung by his obliviousness to the needs of battered women, Inuit or otherwise.

Appeal from such a decision under the current institutional arrangement would not only be unlikely but, for the reasons noted above, it would be compromised for failing to include any Inuit who might respond to an appeal-court judge's declaration: "This is what we do in these circumstances." The voices of women would similarly be silenced.

An appeal circle intending to be an agent of justice as well as an agent of love would need to be wider than the particular community and the particular court personnel. A more fitting institutional appeal structure would have representatives from the relevant collectivities in the appeal.

Recognizing that the Qallunaat, while outsiders in Nuna, are insiders in Nunavik, representatives of the Qallunaat justice system would be appropriate in this wider circle. In narcotics cases such a circle might include those upon whom drug abuse has an impact. In cases of break and enter, it might include those who have been burglarized. In cases of violence against women, it would have representatives of women's interests in Inuit communities. And certainly in appeals from Nunavik sentencing circles, local Inuit should be included to determine whether the Nunavikmiut could feel at home with the decision of first instance.

This circle might indeed be set up in advance to settle on what would constitute a just and an unjust way to proceed, a reasonable and unreasonable use of the trump. Since sentencing circles take place in other than Inuit communities, other Aboriginal groups would be well placed to speak to their own particular concerns, to what they would do in the circumstances. Creating this circle would amount to little more than a formalization of the dialogue already taking place between Pauktuutit, various ministers of Justice, judges, Aboriginal communities, Aboriginal leaders, Royal Commissions, Justice task forces, and individual members of diverse communities.

The order of reflection in this circle would aim to guard against the self-regarding and partial interests of one judge or one community. To this circle, a range of intelligibilities – from the sense that an individual makes of her life to the sense that a culture or a state makes of people's lives – would be brought to bear. Participants would put forward arguments and stories that speak to what constitutes beneficial and what constitutes harmful accommodation of another group's familiar world into one's own. People would be invited to speak about the histories that have emerged within the constraints and injunctions of power, as well as about the pain that such asymmetry has brought about.

This is – current structure of the trump aside – the imagery of the sentencing circle. There is no more essential thing, outside of the accounts brought to the circle, to which reference must be made in determining just outcomes. The visual field has no limits, no wormholes that will permit a kind of perspective on the visual field which is not simultaneously a part of the visual field. By increasing attempts at including the familiar worlds of relevant collectivities, this circle would ruminate "as if" … as if it could grasp the whole range of experiences which make a human life intelligible … as if it could grasp also this moment's grasp.

From these various circles deliberating over time, a custom or practice would emerge. The trials and errors of previous sentencing circles would be used to indicate how to go on in the right direction. The custom would generate criteria for what it would be to make a mistake. The custom would also generate what it would mean for something to be the same as something that has gone before and what it means for something to be different. It would generate criteria for making distinctions between what is in front of the circle now and what has gone before. It would be possible to decide like cases alike. The agreements in judgment that ground the practice of sentencing circles would build an expectation that new circles stand by former practice or justify their departures, a process not dissimilar, of course, to the principle of *stare decisis*. From this practice would emerge a body of common law.[56]

This would be a body of intercultural common law. And while it would be an emerging body of intercultural common law, it would also be an emerging body of Aboriginal common law. To the extent that the Inuit continue to adopt aspects of the southern legal system and familiarize the latter with their context, the sensibility thus generated would be their own. These aspects of the law would speak to the Inuit with authority.

Of course, the implication runs both ways. To the extent that Qallunaat legal sensibilities engage in a reciprocal exchange with Inuit sensibilities and participate in generating this branch of the law, the emerging body of common law would be an extension of Qallunaat common law. Both Qallunaat and Inuit would be plumbing the different interpretive and imaginative possibilities within the shared practices of their respective cultures. But they would also be plumbing the possibilities in the collective resources of the intercultural field upon which they have both been moving since the dialogue began. Such a formalization would allow for the emergence of local knowledge and local justice while providing a mechanism for the transcendence of its sometimes partial and self-regarding nature.

Of course, it is only my own anxieties that have been assuaged by this proposal, and perhaps only temporarily assuaged at that. Undoubtedly there are other anxieties that have not been addressed or recognized. No doubt there are other possibilities for reconciling Qallunaat and Inuit sensibilities. These are narratives waiting to be told.

Notes

NUNAVIK, 1992

1 "L'expression 'flying circus' n'est pas sans affecter grandement les divers intervenants ... La comparaison avec les amuseurs publics n'est plus trouvée drôle par personne et les premiers intéressés n'ont pas l'intention de la voir se perpétuer." Cited in Mylene Jaccoud, "L'administration de Justice au Nouveau-Québec", thèse de doctorat, Université de Montréal, 1993), 157. Recently published as *Justice blanche au Nunavik* (Montréal: Éditions du Méridien, 1995).

INTRODUCTION

1 Martha C. Nussbaum, *Love's Knowledge: Essays on Philosophy and Literature* (New York: Oxford University Press, 1992), 7.

TOPONYMY AND ITS OBJECTS

1 Pierre Bourdieu, *Outline of a Theory of Practice* (Cambridge: Cambridge University Press, 1977), 2.
2 Ludger Müller-Wille, "Place Names, Territoriality and Sovereignty: Inuit Perception of Space in Nunavik (Canadian Eastern Arctic)," *Schweizerische Amerikanisten-Gesellschaft* bull. 53–54 (1989–90), 19.
3 In 1981 the Northern Québec Inuit Elders Conference passed a resolution to institute a project to preserve Inuit place names. In 1983, Avataq Cultural Institute and Indigenous Names Surveys of the Department of Geography, McGill University, implemented the Inuit Place Names Project to collect systematically all Inuit geographical names in the Arctic region

of the Québec-Labrador peninsula. The toponymic maps, as well as a description of surveys and methodology, can be found in the Ludger Müller-Wille, *Gazeteer of Inuit Place Names in Nunavik* (Inoucdjouaq, Québec: Avataq Cultural Institute, 1987), 6–18.

4 Muller-Wille, "The Legacy of Native Toponyms: Towards Establishing the Inuit Place Name Inventory of the Kativik Region (Québec)," *Onamastica Canadiana*, 65 (June 1984), 5.

5 Ibid., 7–8.

6 "The consequences of these absurd limits can be felt also in the domain of policing: in effect, Eskimos who have committed a delict or a crime, tryable before the courts of Québec, could escape from the Québec police simply by taking refuge on an island several hundred metres off the shoreline. What would be required then is that either Québec demand from Ottawa the authorization to pursue an individual liable for arrest, or the mounted police of Frobisher, or of Cap Dorset, travel considerable distances to come and arrest the accused so as to hand the guilty parties to the Québec prosecutors." Author's translation. M. Brochu, *Le défi du Nouveau-Québec* (Montréal: Éditions du Jour, 1962), 19.

7 Hugh Brody, "Permanence and Change among the Inuit and Settlers of Labrador," in Brice-Bennett, Carol, ed., *Our Footprints Are Everywhere: Inuit Land Use and Occupancy in Labrador* (Ottawa: Labrador Inuit Association, 1977), 195.

8 Muller-Wille, "Une méthodologie pour les enquêtes toponymiques autochtones: Le répertoire inuit de la région de Kativik et de sa zone côtière," *Études/Inuit/Studies* 9, no. 1 (1985): 63, and *Our Footprints Are Everywhere*, 195 et seq.

9 Brody, "Permanence and Change among the Inuit and Settlers of Labrador," 318.

10 See, for example, Geoffrey Lester, "Aboriginal Land Rights: The Significance of Inuit Place-Naming," *Études/Inuit/Studies* 3, no. 1 (1979).

11 Nick Hallendy, "The Last Known Traditional Inuit Trial on Southwest Baffin Island in the Canadian Arctic," background paper no. 2 for *Places of Power and Objects of Veneration in the Canadian Arctic*, prepared for the World Archaeological Congress III; appendix: definitions (1994).

12 Brochu, *Le défi du Nouveau-Québec*, 19.

13 "This policy symbolizes the solid determination of the province of Québec to mark its French presence in these new regions." Author's translation. Ibid., 126.

14 See Edwin Rich, *Copy Book of Letters Outward & c, Begins 29th May, 1680 Ends 5 July, 1687* (Toronto: Champlain Society, 1948). I am indebted to

Geoffrey Lester for his interesting synopsis of this historical dispute. See Geoffrey Lester, "Aboriginal Land Rights."

15 Ibid., 286.

16 Ibid., 222, 281.

17 Ibid., 273.

18 Robin Collingwood, *The Idea of History* (Oxford: Clarendon Press, 1945), 246.

19 Ibid., 244.

20 In the Nürnberg trials, the fact of the Holocaust was the background on which the trials of the accused took place. What was proved or disproved was the complicity of the accused in the historical fact. In *R. v. Keegstra*, 19 ccc (3d) 254 (1984), a leading case on point, judicial notice was a central issue in the prosecution of a *holocaust-denier* under Canadian anti-hate laws. If the court failed to take judicial notice of the Holocaust, allowing that its existence was a matter requiring proof, Keegstra was merely questioning what the court allowed was open to speculation. If the court took judicial notice of the Holocaust, his defence was burdened. Against the court's affirmation of what everybody knows, Keegstra's speculations became unconscionable and amounted to hate propaganda.

21 Technical Paper No. 14 (Montreal: Arctic Institute of North America, 1964), 128.

22 Thomas Correll, "Language and Location in Traditional Inuit Societies," in Milton M.R. Freeman, ed., *Report: Inuit Land Use and Occupancy Project* (Ottawa: Department of Supply and Services, 1976), vol. 2, 174.

23 The suffix "*-miut*" means "the people of" or "the inhabitants of." Each *miut* group is distinguished from another by differences in dialect and identification with a certain general territory. Members of a *miut* group consider themselves to be related, and (in the traditional period) each *miut* group consisted of a cluster of camps or settlements that formed the central polity of the group. See Correll, ibid., 173.

24 Bernard Saladin d'Anglure, "Inuit of Quebec," *Handbook of North American Indians* (Washington: Smithsonian Institute Press, 1991) vol. 5, *Arctic*, 477.

25 Ibid., 480; Keith Crowe, *A History of the Original Peoples of Northern Canada* (Montréal: Arctic Institute of North America, 1974), 17.

26 M. Mauss, "A Category of the Human Mind: The Notion of Person; The Notion of Self," in *The Category of the Person*, Carrithers, M., ed. (New York: Cambridge University Press, 1985), 22.

27 Saladin D'Anglure, "Inuit of Quebec," *Handbook of North American Indians*, vol. 5, 476.

28 Edward Adamson Hoebel, *The Law of Primitive Man: A Study in Comparative Legal Dynamics* (Cambridge: Harvard University Press, 1954), 70.

29 Kit Minor, *Issumatuq: Learning from the Traditional Healing Wisdom of the Canadian Inuit* (Halifax: Fernwood Publishing, 1992), 39.

30 Ibid., 37.

31 Ibid., 37.

32 A. Fienup-Riordan, "The Real People: The Concept of Personhood among the Yup'ik Eskimos of Western Alaska," *Études/Inuit/Studies*, 10 (1–2) (1986): 262.

33 Brice-Bennett, *Our Footprints Are Everywhere*, 114.

34 See J. Cruikshank, *When the World Began* (Yukon Territory: Department of Education, Government of Yukon Territory, 1978)

35 Crowe, *A History of the Original Peoples of Northern Canada*, 17.

36 Saladin d'Anglure, "Inuit of Quebec," 496.

37 Ludwig Wittgenstein, *On Certainty* (New York: Harper, 1969), paras. 97, 99.

38 Jeremy Webber has eloquently argued for this understanding of reciprocity in his article "Rapports de force, rapports de justice: la genèse d'une communauté normative entre colonisateurs et colonisés," in J.-G. Belley, ed., *Le droit soluble: contributions québécoises à l'étude de l'internormativité* (Paris: LGDJ, 1995).

39 Jenness, "Eskimo Administration," 14.

40 Ibid., 102–3.

41 SCR 104 [1939] (hereinafter *Re Eskimos*).

42 This agreement was summarized in the international law case *Island of Palmas Case*, 2 R.I.A.A. (1928), 829.

43 W. Morrison, "Canadian Sovereignty and the Inuit of the Central and Eastern Arctic," *Études/Inuit/Studies*, 10, no. 1–2 (1986): 246.

44 Frank James Tester and Peter Kulchyski, *Tammarniit: Inuit Relocation in the Eastern Arctic, 1939–63* (Vancouver: University of Britsh Columbia Press, 1994).

45 Saladin d'Anglure, "Inuit of Quebec," 476.

46 Mylene Jaccoud, "L'administration de Justice au Nouveau-Québec" (thèse de doctorat, Université de Montréal, 1993), 112. I am indebted to Jaccoud for her original research and analysis of the history of the legal system in Nunavik.

47 A. Goyette, "L'Administration de la justice au Nouveau-Québec Inuit: de l'évolution d'une justice imposée" (thèse de maîtrise, Faculté des sciences sociales, Université Laval, 1987), 74.

48 Saladin d'Anglure, "Inuit of Quebec," 685.

49 Jaccoud, "L'administration de Justice au Nouveau-Québec," 113.

50 (Que sc) (1973).

51 *Société de Développment de la Baie James et Autres* c. *Chef Robert Kanate-wat et autres,* CA 166 [1975], 177, 178.

52 As Natives were taken to have "evolved rapidly towards a way of life which is that of all Quebeckers," the interests of the Québec population included those of the Natives. Author's translation. Ibid.

53 James Bay and Northern Québec Agreement (Québec: Editeur officiel du Québec, 1976).

54 John Ciacca, MNA, remarking on the philosophy of the agreement, preface to the James Bay Agreement, XXI.

55 Morrison, "Canadian Sovereignty and the Inuit of the Central and Eastern Arctic," 247.

56 Henry Larson, "Patrolling the Arctic and the Northwest Passage in the R.C.M.P. Ship St. Roch – 1944" (Ottawa: Department of Northern Affairs and National Resources, 1944), 2.

57 See page 47.

58 Jaccoud, "L'Administration de Justice au Nouveau-Québec," 100.

59 Cited in Morrison, "Canadian Sovereignty and the Inuit of the Central and Eastern Arctic," 251.

60 George Binney, *The Eskimo Book of Knowledge* (London: Hudson's Bay Company, 1931), 60–2.

61 The Inuit only became predominantly sedentary in the 1950s with the intro-duction of family-allowance cheques and schooling. Prior to this their trap-ping routines took them onto the land during the trapping season and brought them tangentially to the trading posts, primarily to trade. See Gérard Duhaime, "La catastrophe et l'État. Histoire démographique et changements sociaux dans l'Arctique," *Études/Inuit/Studies* 7, no. 2 (1989): 25.

62 Goyette, "L'Administration de la justice au Nouveau-Québec Inuit," 37.

63 "Only the group allows the individual to live. The individual, so protected, reserves, in return, for the society, his energy and his thoughts. To the point that, repressing all individual reaction, he only expresses himself in the third person, the merger of a general conception, that of the group. Never does an Eskimo say: I think, but the Inuit think." Author's transla-tion. J. Malaurie, "Raids et esclavage dans les sociétés autochtones du détroit de Behring," in *Inter-Nord,* 13–14 (Dec. 1974): 153.

64 Jean Briggs, *Never in Anger: Portrait of an Eskimo Family* (Cambridge: Har-vard University Press, 1970), 4.

65 Ibid., 3.

66 "At the level of legal sanction, this sociological principle has the effect that public opinion plays a preponderant role in the application of procedures designed to rectify deviant behaviour. Expressing the judgment of the group – that which certain wise individuals can help to release – that is supreme." Author's translation. N. Rouland, "Les modes juridiques de solution des conflits chez les Inuit," *Études/Inuit/Studies* 3, supplementary issue (1976): 21.

67 Briggs, *Never in Anger*, 64.

68 "The group, directly or by the intermediary of certain authorities, intervenes very actively in the process of legal constraint, either in setting limitations to the private means of solving conflicts in the name of public interest, or in putting in place true types of public action." Author's translation. Rouland, "Les modes juridiques...": 9.

69 Asen Balikci, *The Netsilik Eskimo* (Garden City: Natural History Press, 1970), 185 et seq.; Hoebel, "Law-ways of the Primitive Eskimos," *Journal of the American Institute of Criminal Law and Criminology* 31 (1941): 663–83; Hoebel, *The Law of Primitive Man*, 70.

70 Hoebel, "Law-ways of the Primitive Eskimos," 670; Balikci, *The Netsilik Eskimo*, 147 et seq.

71 Hoebel, "Law-ways of the Primitive Eskimos" and *The Law of Primitive Man*; Balikci, *The Netsilik Eskimo*.

72 Duhaime, "La sédentarisation au Nouveau-Québec inuit," *Études/Inuit/Studies* 7, no. 2 (1983): 38.

73 Nelson Graburn, *Eskimos without Igloos: Social and Economic Development in Sugluk* (Boston: Little Brown, 1969), 49.

74 Public Archives of Canada, Record Group 85, vol. 1870, file 540-1, Cory to Gibson, June 22, 1945; cited in A. Goyette, "L'Administration de la justice au Nouveau-Québec Inuit," 69.

75 Public Archives of Canada; cited in Goyette, ibid., 68.

76 In 1921 the RCMP commented on "the totally primitive conditions in which these Aboriginals live and their ignorance of the laws." Author's translation. RCMP Commissioner's Report, 1921, 20; cited in Goyette, 35.

77 Public Archives of Canada, Record Group 85, vol. 175, file 541-2-1, also cited in Goyette, 50.

78 Ibid., 53.

79 Ibid., 54.

80 Jaccoud, "L'Administration de Justice au Nouveau-Québec," 112.

81 Ibid., 115.

82 S. Bouchard and C. Pelletier, *La Justice en question: Évaluation de projets de création d'un comité de justice à Povungnituk* (Montreal: Centre de recherche et d'analyse en sciences humaines, 1986), 13.

83 Jerome Choquette, *The Administration of Justice beyond the 50th Parallel* (Québec: no publisher cited, 1973), 42.

84 Ibid., 41.

85 The central complaint of the Inuit was that the bill cut the Inuit of Québec off from their counterparts in the rest of the circumpolar region whose second language was English. Their main demand was for control over the pace at which French replaced English as the second language of the area. The dispute was resolved by the provincial government conceding to this demand and assuring the Inuit that the language laws were not intended to supplant Inuit language and culture. *MacLean's* 90 (1977): 20–1.

86 S. Bouchard and C. Pelletier, *La Justice en question*, 17.

87 The report *La Justice en question: Évaluation de projets de création d'un comité de justice à Povungnituk*, ibid.

88 *Cour Itinérante* (August 1986), cited in Jaccoud, "L'Administration de Justice au Nouveau-Québec," 155.

89 *Blazing the Trail to a Better Future, Inuit Justice Task Force Final Report* (Montréal: Makivik, 1993), 58, 64, 60.

90 Ibid., 118.

91 Ibid., 66, 61, 70.

92 He speculated whether "it was not preferable to leave to these people the ability to regulate between themselves problems of a criminal nature." Author's translation. Jean-Charles Coutu, "La cour itinérante du district d'Abiti." *Bulletin canadien de l'aide juridique* 5, no. 1 (1982): 25.

LOVERS AND HEALING CIRCLES

1 Müller-Wille, *Gazeteer of Inuit Place Names in Nunavik*, 14.

2 Saladin d'Anglure, "Inuit of Quebec," 492.

3 An umiak is a skin boat.

4 One of the Native police officers speculated in 1992 that persistent family violence was common in 85 per cent of the homes in Kuujjuaq and occasional family violence in another 10 per cent.

5 Hoebel, *The Law of Primitive Man: A Study in Comparative Legal Dynamics*, 86.

6 Peter Freuchen, *Arctic Adventure: My Life in the Frozen North* (New York: Farrar and Rinehart, 1935), 297–9.

7 Hoebel, *The Law of Primitive Man*, 83.

8 Knud Rasmussen, *Across Arctic America* (New York: Putnam's Sons, 1927), 250.

9 Hoebel, *The Law of Primitive Man*, 83–4.

10 Rasmussen, *Across Arctic America*, 60–1, cited in Hoebel, *The Law of Primitive Man*, 85–6.

11 Nitya Duclos, "Lessons of Difference: Feminist Theory on Cultural Diversity," *Buffalo Law Review* 38, no. 2 (1990): 367–8.

12 *Natural Parents* v. *The Superintendent of Child Welfare et al.* 2 SCR 751 [1976] and *Racine* v. *Woods* 2 SCR 173 [1983] (hereinafter *Racine*).

13 *Racine*, 186.

14 Erik Erikson, *Identity, Youth and Crisis* (New York: W.W. Norton, 1968), 308.

15 Toni Morrison, *Beloved* (New York: Plume, 1987), 251.

16 Erikson, *Identity, Youth and Crisis*, 25.

17 Wittgenstein, *Philosophical Investigations* (Oxford: Basil Blackwell, 1978), §32.

18 Remark made by McGill anthropology professor Toby Morantz, in Aboriginal Peoples and the Law class, McGill University, March, 1992.

19 Wittgenstein, *On Certainty* (Anthony Kenny has collated these latter aphorisms from Wittgenstein's *On Certainty*, §310–15 and §160.

20 *Communities in Crisis: Healing Ourselves* (Montréal: Waseskun House, 1991).

21 Ibid.

22 Erikson, *Identity, Youth and Crisis*, 297.

23 Ibid., 297.

24 Simone Weil, *The Need for Roots* (London: Routledge & Kegan Paul, 1952).

25 *Communities in Crisis*, conference transcripts.

26 Peter Winch, *Simone Weil: "The Just Balance"* (Cambridge: Cambridge University Press, 1989), 182.

27 A more exact reference cannot be given due to the confidential nature of the healing circle.

28 Richard Rorty, *Contingency, Irony, and Solidarity* (Cambridge: Cambridge University Press, 1989), 37.

29 Jeremy Webber used phrasing similar to this in his class Social Diversity and the Law at McGill University's Faculty of Law. This way of framing the tensions that individuals feel as members of different and diverse communities arises again in his book *Reimagining Canada: Language, Culture, Community, and the Canadian Constitution* (Montréal: McGill-Queen's University Press, 1994) and is persuasively and elegantly elaborated.

30 Nussbaum, "The Speech of Alcibiades," *Philosophy and Literature*, vol. 3, no. 1 (1979): 140.

31 Ibid., 140.

32 Morrison, *Beloved*, 272–3.

33 Nussbaum, "The Speech of Alcibiades," 140.

34 Paula Gunn Allen and Emma LaRoque in *Report of the Aboriginal Justice Inquiry of Manitoba*, vol. 1: The Justice System of Aboriginal People, (Manitoba: Manitoba Department of Justice, December 1991), 479–80.

35 Louise Erdrich, *Love Medicine* (New York: Holt, Rinehart and Winston, 1984), 16–42 (specifically 16, 17, 17, 24, 42).

36 Account of Dominican priests in the Carribean, cited in Thomas Berger, *A Long and Terrible Shadow* (Vancouver: Douglas & McIntyre, 1991), 5.

37 Weil, "Human Personality" in *Simone Weil: An Anthology*, ed. Siân Miles (London: Virago Press, 1986); cited in Peter Winch, *Simone Weil: "The Just Balance,"* 182.

AGENTS OF JUSTICE/AGENTS OF LOVE

1 Canadian Criminal Code, s. 717(1).

2 *Sentencing Reform: A Canadian Approach*, Report of the Canadian Sentencing Commission (Ottawa: Minister of Supply and Services Canada, 1987), 72.

3 See, for example, *R. v. Sandercock* (1985), 22 CCC (3d) 79 (Alta CA).

4 Ibid., 80.

5 Wittgenstein, *Philosophical Investigations* (Oxford, Basil Blackwell, 1978), §99.

6 *R. v. Fireman*, 3 OR 380 (CA) [1971], 383.

7 Wittgenstein, *Philosophical Investigations*, §85.

8 Ibid., §198.

9 Ibid., §201.

10 Ibid., §217.

11 Ibid., §198.

12 Peter Winch, *The Idea of a Social Science* (London: Routledge & Kegan Paul, 1958) 30–1.

13 Wittgenstein, *Philosophical Investigations*, §85.

14 Bourdieu, *Outline of a Theory of Practice* (Cambridge: Cambridge University Press, 1993), 78, 166, 80, 3.

15 Wittgenstein, *Philosophical Investigations*, §88.

16 Bourdieu, *Outline of a Theory of Practice*, 164.

17 Clifford Geertz, *The Interpretation of Cultures* (New York: Basic Books, 1973), 14.

18 René David and John Brierley, *Major Legal Systems in the World Today* (London: Stevens and Sons, 1985), 550.

19 G. Pitcher, *The Philosophy of Wittgenstein* (New Jersey: Prentice-Hall, 1964), 221.

20 David and Brierley, *Major Legal Systems in the World Today*, 21.

21 Wittgenstein, *Philosophical Investigations*, §66.

22 Ibid., §66–67.

23 Ibid., §68.

24 Ibid., §71.

25 Ibid., §69.

26 Ibid.

27 Ibid.

28 Ibid., §67.

29 Ibid., paraphrase of §381: "How do I know that this colour is red? – It would be an answer to say: 'I have learnt English'."

30 Ibid., §75.

31 Ibid.

32 Wittgenstein, *On Certainty*, §152.

33 Wittgenstein, *Philosophical Investigations*, §6.

34 Ibid., §69.

35 Geertz, "Local Knowledge: Fact and Law in Comparative Perspective," in *Local Knowledge: Further Essays in Interpretive Anthropology* (New York: Basic Books, 1983), 221.

36 S. Vincent, "Background and Beginnings," *James Bay and Northern Québec: Ten Years After,* ed. Sylvie Vincent, Garry Bowers (Québec: Recherches Amérindiennes au Québec, 1988), 211.

37 Saladin D'Anglure, "Contemporary Inuit of Québec," *Handbook of North American Indians* (Washington: Smithsonian Institute, 1982), 685.

38 Paul Veyne, *Comment on écrit l'histoire* (France: Éditions du Seuil, 1971), cited in Vincent, "Background and Beginnings," 211.

39 Norman Malcolm, *Thought and Knowledge* (Ithaca and London: Cornell University Press, 1977), 200.

40 Rorty, "On Ethnocentrism: A Reply to Clifford Geertz," *Michigan Quarterly Review* 25, no. 3 (Summer 1986): 525.

41 I am grateful to Jobi Tukiapik and Louisa Whiteley of Kuujjuaq for their contributions to this example.

42 Fieldnotes, Kuujjuaq, 1993.

43 Rorty, "On Ethnocentrism," 529.

44 "You should know therefore that if one of your people is accused of committing a serious crime against the Laws … *on no account* should that man be punished by your people in any way … For … if you punish that man you are also guilty of a crime and you are likely also to be punished for breaking the Law." Binney, *The Eskimo Book of Knowledge* (London: Hudson's Bay Company, 1931), 60–2, cited in "Toponymy and Its Objects," 52.

45 71 CCC (3d) 347 (Yukon Terr. Ct.) (1992) [hereinafter *Moses*].

46 Iris Murdoch, *The Sovereignty of Good* (London: Routledge and Kegan Paul, 1970), 20.

47 *Moses*, 358.

48 Fieldnotes, Community C, Nunavik, May 1993.

49 Mary Crnkovich, *Report on the Sentencing Circle in Nunavik* (Pauktuutit and Department of Justice, Canada, 1993), 16, 10.

50 Ibid., 17, 24.

51 Ibid., 6.

52 Ibid., 24.

53 Fieldnotes, Kuujjuaq, May 1993.

54 Ibid.

55 Judge Dutil, written reasons for judgment in Nunavik's first sentencing circle, May 1993.

56 I am grateful to James Tully and Natalie Oman for assistance in developing these ideas. See also Jeremy Webber, "Rapports de force, rapports de justice: la genèse d'une communauté normative entre colonisateurs et colonisés."

Bibliography

Balikci, A. *The Netsilik Eskimo.* Garden City: Natural History Press 1970.

Berger, T. *A Long and Terrible Shadow.* Vancouver: Douglas & McIntyre 1991.

Binney, G. *The Eskimo Book of Knowledge.* London: Hudson's Bay Company 1931.

Boas, F. "The Eskimo of Baffin Land and Hudson Bay." *Bulletin of the American Museum of Natural History,* 15, 1907.

Bouchard, S., and C. Pelletier, *La Justice en question: Evaluation de projets de création d'un comité de justice à Povungnituk.* Montreal: Centre de recherche et d'analyse en sciences humaines (ssDcc inc) 1986.

Bourdieu, P. *Outline of a Theory of Practice.* Cambridge: Cambridge University Press 1977.

Brice-Bennett, C., ed. *Our Footprints Are Everywhere: Inuit Land Use and Occupancy in Labrador.* Ottawa: Labrador Inuit Association 1977.

Briggs, J. *Never in Anger: Portrait of an Eskimo Family.* Cambridge: Harvard University Press 1970.

Brochu, M. *Le défi du Nouveau-Québec.* Montreal: Éditions du Jour 1962.

Brody, H. "Permanence and Change among the Inuit and Settlers of Labrador," in Brice-Bennett, C., ed., *Our Footprints Are Everywhere: Inuit Land Use and Occupancy in Labrador.* Ottawa: Labrador Inuit Association 1977.

Collingwood, R. *The Idea of History.* Oxford: Clarendon Press 1945.

Correll, T. "Language and Location in Traditional Inuit Societies," in Milton M.R. Freeman, ed., *Report: Inuit Land Use and Occupancy Project,* vol. 2. Ottawa: Department of Supply and Services 1976.

Coutu, J.-C. "La cour itinérante du district d'Abiti." *Bulletin canadien de l'aide juridique* 5, no. 1 (1982).

Crnkovich, M. *Report on the Sentencing Circle in Nunavik.* Pauktuutit and Department of Justice, Canada 1993.

Crowe, K. *A History of the Original Peoples of Northern Canada.* Montreal: Arctic Institute of North America 1974.

Cruikshank, J. *When the World Began.* Yukon Territory: Department of Education, Government of Yukon Territory 1978.

David, R., and J. Brierley. *Major Legal Systems in the World Today.* London: Stevens and Sons 1985.

Dillard, A. *An American Childhood.* New York: Harper and Row 1987.

Duclos, N. "Lessons of Difference: Feminist Theory on Cultural Diversity." *Buffalo Law Review* 38, no. 2 (1990).

Duhaime, G. "La catastrophe et l'État. Histoire démographique et changements sociaux dans l'Arctique." *Études/Inuit/Studies* 13, no. 2 (1989).

– "La sédentarisation au Nouveau-Québec inuit." *Études/Inuit/Studies* 7, no. 2 (1983).

Erdrich, L. *Love Medicine.* New York: Holt, Rinehart and Winston 1984.

Erikson, E. *Identity, Youth and Crisis.* New York: W.W. Norton 1968.

Fienup-Riordan, A. "The Real People: The Concept of Personhood among the Yup'ik Eskimos of Western Alaska." *Études/Inuit/Studies* 10 (1–2) (1986).

Freuchen, P. *Arctic Adventure: My Life in the Frozen North.* New York: Farrar and Rinehart 1935.

Geertz, C. *The Interpretation of Cultures.* New York: Basic Books 1973.

– "Local Knowledge: Fact and Law in Comparative Perspective," in *Local Knowledge: Further Essays in Interpretive Anthropology.* New York: Basic Books 1983.

Goyette, A. "L'Administration de la justice au Nouveau-Québec Inuit: de l'évolution d'une justice imposée." Thèse de maîtrise, Faculté des sciences sociales, Université Laval.

Graburn, N. *Eskimos without Igloos: Social and Economic Development in Sugluk.* Boston: Little Brown 1969.

Hallendy, N. "The Last Known Traditional Inuit Trial on Southwest Baffin Island in the Canadian Arctic." Background Paper No. 2 for *Places of Power and Objects of Veneration in the Canadian Arctic,* prepared for the World Archaeological Congress III (1994).

Hoebel, E.A. "Law-ways of the Primitive Eskimos." *Journal of Criminology and Criminal Law* (1941).

– *The Law of Primitive Man: A Study in Comparative Legal Dynamics.* Cambridge: Harvard University Press 1964.

Jaccoud, M. "L'Administration de justice au Nouveau-Québec." Thèse de doctorat, Université de Montréal (1993).

Jenness, D. *Eskimo Administration,* Technical Paper No. 14. Montreal: Arctic Institute of North America 1964.

Kenny, A. *Wittgenstein.* Suffolk: Penguin Press 1973.

Larson, H. "Patrolling the Arctic and the Northwest Passage in the R.C.M.P. Ship St. Roch – 1944." Ottawa: Department of Northern Affairs and National Resources 1944.

Lester, G. "Aboriginal Land Rights: The Significance of Inuit Place-Naming." *Études/Inuit/Studies* 3, no. 1 (1979).

Malaurie, J. "Raids et esclavage dans les sociétés autochtones du détroit de Behring." *Inter-Nord* 13–14 (Dec. 1974).

Malcolm, N. *Thought and Knowledge.* Ithaca and London: Cornell University Press 1977.

Mauss, M. "A Category of the Human Mind: The Notion of Person; the Notion of Self," in *The Category of the Person,* Carrithers, M., ed. New York: Cambridge University Press 1985.

Minor, K. *Issumatuq: Learning from the Traditional Healing Wisdom of the Canadian Inuit.* Halifax: Fernwood Publishing 1992.

Morrison, T. *Beloved.* New York: Plume 1987.

Morrison, W. "Canadian Sovereignty and the Inuit of the Central and Eastern Arctic." *Études/Inuit/Studies* 10, no. 1–2 (1986).

Müller-Wille, L. *Gazeteer of Inuit Place Names in Nunavik.* Inoucdjouaq, Québec: Avataq Cultural Institute 1987.

– "The Legacy of Native Toponyms: Towards Establishing the Inuit Place Name Inventory of the Kativik Region (Québec)." *Onamastica Canadiana* 65 (June 1984).

– "Une méthodologie pour les enquêtes toponymiques autochtones: Le répertoire inuit de la région de Kativik et de sa zone côtière." *Études/Inuit/Studies* 9, no. 1 (1985).

– "Place Names, Territoriality and Sovereignty: Inuit Perception of Space in Nunavik (Canadian Eastern Arctic)." *Schweizerische Amerikanisten-Gesellschaft,* Bull. 53–54 (1989–90).

Murdoch, I. *The Sovereignty of Good.* London: Routledge and Kegan Paul 1970.

Nussbaum, M.C. *Love's Knowledge: Essays on Philosophy and Literature.* New York: Oxford University Press 1992.

– "The Speech of Alcibiades." *Philosophy and Literature* 3, no. 1 (Spring 1979).

Pitcher, G. *The Philosophy of Wittgenstein.* New Jersey: Prentice-Hall 1964.

Rasmussen, K. *Across Arctic America.* New York: Putnam's Sons 1927.

Rich, E. *Copy Book of Letters Outward & c, Begins 29th May, 1680 Ends 5 July, 1687.* Toronto: Champlain Society 1948.

Rorty, R. *Contingency, Irony, and Solidarity.* Cambridge: Cambridge University Press 1989.

– "On Ethnocentrism: A Reply to Clifford Geertz." *Michigan Quarterly Review* 25, no. 3 (Summer 1986).

Rouland, N. "Les modes juridiques de solution des conflits chez les Inuit."
    Études/Inuit/Studies 3, supplementary issue (1976).

Saladin d'Anglure, B. "Inuit of Quebec." *Handbook of North American Indians,*
    vol. 5, *Arctic.* Washington: Smithsonian Institute Press 1991.

Tester, F.J. and P. Kulchyski. *Tammarniit: Inuit Relocation in the Eastern Arctic,*
    1939–63. Vancouver: University of Britsh Columbia Press 1994.

Vincent, S. "Background and Beginnings," in *James Bay and Northern Québec:*
    Ten Years After, ed. Sylvie Vincent, Garry Bowers. Québec: Recherches Amé-
    rindiennes au Québec 1988.

Webber, J. "Rapports de force, rapports de justice: la genèse d'une communauté
    normative entre colonisateurs et colonisés," in J.-G. Belley, ed., *Le droit solu-*
    ble: contributions québécoises à l'étude de l'internormativité. Paris: LGDJ 1995.

– *Reimagining Canada: Language, Culture, Community, and the Canadian Con-*
    stitution. Montréal: McGill-Queen's University Press 1994.

Weil, S. "Human Personality" in *Simone Weil: An Anthology,* ed Siân Miles.
    London: Virago Press 1986.

– *The Need for Roots.* London: Routledge & Kegan Paul 1952.

Winch, P. *The Idea of a Social Science.* London: Routledge & Kegan Paul 1958.

– *Simone Weil: "The Just Balance."* Cambridge: Cambridge University Press
    1989.

Wittgenstein, L. *On Certainty.* New York: Harper 1969.

Wittgenstein, L. *Philosophical Investigations.* Oxford: Basil Blackwell 1978.

Wittgenstein, L. *Zettel.* California: University of California Press 1970.

REPORTS

Aboriginal Peoples and Criminal Justice: Equality, Respect and the Search for Jus-
    tice. Ottawa: Law Reform Commission of Canada 1991.

Blazing the Trail to a Better Future: Inuit Justice Task Force Final Report. Mont-
    réal: Makivik 1993.

Choquette, J. *The Administration of Justice beyond the 50th Parallel.* Québec: no
    publisher cited, 1973.

Communities in Crisis: Healing Ourselves. Montréal: Waseskun House 1991.

Drummond, S., and L. Whiteley, eds. *Family Violence in Kuujjuaq: Talking to*
    Each Other. Kuujjuaq: Kuujjuaq Social Services 1992.

Manitoba Justice Inquiry. Manitoba: Manitoba Department of Justice, December
    1991.

Sentencing Reform: A Canadian Approach. Report of the Canadian Sentencing
    Commission. Ottawa: Minister of Supply and Services Canada 1987.

The Inuit Way: A Guide to Inuit Culture. Ottawa: Pauktuutit 1990.

CASES

Island of Palmas Case, 2 R.I.A.A. (1928).

James Bay and Northern Québec Agreement. Québec: Éditeur officiel du Québec 1976.

Kanatewat v. James Bay Development Corporation (Que sc) (1973).

MacLean's 90 (1977): 20–1.

Natural Parents v. The Superintendent of Child Welfare et al. 2 SCR 751 [1976].

R. v. Fireman, 3 OR 380 (CA) [1971].

R. v. Keegstra, 19 CCC (3d) 254 (1984).

R. v. Moses, 71 CCC (3d) 347 (Yukon Terr. Ct.) (1992).

R. v. Sandercock, 22 CCC (3d) 79 (Alta CA) (1985).

Racine v. Woods, 2 SCR 173 [1983].

Re Eskimos, SCR 104 [1939].

Société de Développpment de la Baie James et Autres c. Chef Robert Kanatewat et autres, CA 166 [1975].

Index